Emily Walker's **A Cook's Tour** *of Nova Scotia*

*A potpourri of facts, fare
treats and trivia*

Emily Walker's A Cook's Tour of Nova Scotia

NIMBUS PUBLISHING LIMITED

© 1987, Emily Ellen Walker

Second Printing 1988

All rights reserved. No part of this publication may be reproduced or transmitted in any form or by any means, electronic or mechanical, including photocopying, recording or any information storage and retrieval system, without the prior written permission of the publisher.

Published by: Nimbus Publishing Limited
 P.O. Box 9301, Station A
 Halifax, N.S. B3K 5N5

Illustrations: J.W. Johnson
Design: J.W. Johnson
Typesetting: Atlantic Typesetting Studio
Printing and Binding: Seaboard Printing

Canadian Cataloguing in Publication Data

Walker, Emily, 1952-
A cook's tour of Nova Scotia

Includes index.
Bibliography: p.
ISBN 0-920852-70-X

1. Cookery, Canadian — Nova Scotia style.
I. Title.

TX715.W32 1987   641.59716   C87-090076-5

Printed and bound in Canada

Introduction

Food and its preparation have been enduring passions with me for as long as I can remember. As a child I took a great interest in the mysterious operations of my mother's busy farm kitchen and was delighted when she encouraged me to try my hand at various cooking tasks.

Notwithstanding major disasters and minor triumphs, I have progressed along the rocky road of trial and error, experimentation and innovation that encounters the self-taught cook. For many years, I dreamed of writing a cookbook but it was not until my husband suggested an historical theme that I embarked on the research project which culminated in *A Cook's Tour of Nova Scotia*.

Intensely proud to be Canadian, I feel particularly fortunate to be a native of Nova Scotia, a province of rare physical beauty and rich in cultural heritage.

My goals in writing this book soon became twofold: to share some of the best recipes in my collection and to inspire the reader's interest in Nova Scotia's history, her people and her achievements.

Linking recipes with particular Nova Scotian communities was an enjoyable exercise whose outcome is a combination of light-hearted fun and a serious tribute to that community's contribution to Nova Scotia. However, the connection between recipe and community is secondary to my aim of presenting simple, elegant recipes and interesting, unusual trivia items garnered from a variety of sources.

I hope *A Cook's Tour of Nova Scotia* brings you many hours of pleasure for both body and spirit.

Codes at the end of a recipe indicate that the recipe can be prepared more efficiently by using a food processor or blender, cooked in a microwave or frozen with good results.

B	Blender	FP	Food Processor
F	Freezer	M	Microwave Oven

For my husband, Rob, whose encouragement and support helped make a dream come true.

With special thanks to friends and family who generously contributed treasured recipes for this book.

Contents

Introduction	
Starters and Appetizers	1
Accompaniments (including breads, muffins, vegetable and cereal dishes)	29
Main Courses	59
Sweets and Desserts	85
Recipe Index	123
Place Name Index	129
List of Illustrations	133
Bibliography	135

Starters & Appetizers

Antigonish

THIS UNUSUAL PLACENAME IS DERIVED FROM A MICMAC phrase meaning "a place where the branches are torn off the trees by bears getting beech nuts."

St. Francis Xavier University, named after the patron saint of Canada, was the first Catholic college in North America to grant degrees to female students. Among the many of its graduates who went on to become successful in the political arena is the Right Honourable Brian Mulroney, Prime Minister of Canada.

Organized in Antigonish in 1929, the *Coady International Institute* has been a driving force behind the formation of co-ops and credit unions in Nova Scotia. The Institute has also played a crucial role in providing training for Canadian and foreign students in adult education. These students have influenced the social order and helped improve the standard of living in Asia, Africa, the Caribbean and Latin America.

The first set of Scottish Highland Games held in Antigonish took place in 1863. Combining Scottish sports and dancing with a distinctively Old Country flavour, the Games are still held every July and are very popular with tourists and locals alike.

Antigonish has been the home of one of Canada's oldest continuing weekly newspapers — *The Casket* — since 1852. This rather peculiar name for a newspaper seems more suitable when it is realized that the word "casket" means a chest of jewels, not a coffin.

Bayfield, an Antigonish County community east of Antigonish takes its name from the famous cartographer Admiral Henry Wolsay Bayfield (1795-1885) who did pioneer work in mapping most of the Nova Scotian mainland, Cape Breton, Prince Edward Island, the Gulf of St. Lawrence and the Great Lakes.

Prince Edward Islander Ken Fraser was extremely pleased with his 1,496-pound bluefin tuna which he caught in *Auld Cove* in 1979. This record-breaking catch would make one big pile of tuna sandwiches!

Guysborough native Henry Marshall Tory (1864-1947) was the first president of the University of Alberta (1920-1928) and the founder and first president of Carleton University (1942-47).

Bayfield Ripe Tomatoes at Their Best
(serves 4)

This is absolutely the best way to serve fresh, red-ripe tomatoes. Both the basil and mayonnaise serve to enhance the natural flavour of tomatoes.

4 tomatoes, medium size, fresh garden ripened
4 tbsp. mayonnaise, good quality* 60 ml
4 tbsp. basil leaves, fresh, chopped 60 ml

*Make sure you are using a good quality mayonnaise. My personal preference is for Hellman's or a good homemade kind.

Slice tomatoes and arrange in a circle on a small salad plate. Place 1 tbsp. (15 ml) of mayonnaise in the centre of each plate. Sprinkle 1 tbsp (15 ml) of finely chopped basil over the tomato slices and mayonnaise.

Canning

AT ONE TIME REFERRED TO BY THE CHARMING TITLE OF "Apple Tree Landing," this little village was renamed in 1830 in honour of George Canning, who served as British Prime Minister in 1827.

The right Honourable John Diefenbaker, a staunch Canadian, Progressive Conservative, and Prime Minister of Canada from 1957 to 1963, has a connection with Canning. His second wife's mother, Angie A. Eaton, cousin of Cyrus Eaton, was born there.

Nearby **Port Williams** had the first commercial gas storage facility for apples in North America. It was built by George A. Chase in 1936. H.C. Aitken developed Canada's first vitaminized apple juice in Chase's processing plant. Born in Port Williams in 1851, William Henry Chase earned the title of the "Apple King of Nova Scotia" for his contributions to the fruit industry. Chase is also remembered for providing the funding for the original Public Archives of Nova Scotia. Built on land contributed by Dalhousie University and designed by architect Andrew Cobb, this was the first building erected specifically to house archival material in Nova Scotia. It opened its doors in 1931.

Just a few miles drive from Canning is the spectacular **Blomidon Lookoff**, affording a panoramic view of the Annapolis Valley. **Cape Blomidon** which soars 760 feet in the air at the end of a 120-mile-ridge (North Mountain), is a beloved landmark and it is said its name came from sailors who called this jutting point "Blow Me Down Cape."

Another point of interest in this area of Kings County is the Prescott House. Charles Ramage Prescott, who is credited with introducing the highly successful Gravenstein apple to Nova Scotia, was a prosperous merchant and keen horticulturist. Prescott House, a fine example of Georgian architecture, has been restored to its early nineteenth century splendour, and the gardens are quite remarkable.

Canning Chicken Liver Pâté

This particularly smooth and tasty pâté is a classic.

3 tbsp. butter *45 ml*
1 medium onion, chopped
1 medium apple, peeled and chopped
1 lb. chicken livers *450 g*
1 tsp. thyme *5 ml*
2 tbsp. brandy or sherry *30 ml*
salt and pepper to taste
¼ lb butter *115 g*

Melt the butter in a pan and sauté the onion and apple until fork tender. Remove the apples and onion from the pan with slotted spoon. Sauté the livers in the same butter, seasoning with salt, pepper and thyme. Stirring gently, cook about 5 minutes, until most of the pinkness has disappeared. Do not overcook.

Remove from the heat, add brandy or sherry and combine this mixture with the chopped onion and apple. Cool for 10 minutes. Cream the butter in a blender or food processor and add the liver mixture. Blend until smooth. Put in crocks and cover tightly with plastic wrap. Refrigerate until ready to use. This pâté freezes well.

Garnish the pâté lightly with sliced stuffed olives, sprigs of parsley or chopped green onion. Serve with crackers, melba toast or small triangles of dark rye bread.

Note: Do not substitute margarine for butter.

B FP F

Clementsport

LOCATED AT THE MOUTH OF MOOSE RIVER, THE SMALL community of Clementsport was the birthplace of wrestler Clark Davis (1956) who was the Olympic silver medalist in 1982.
Although the Carter family home is now in Port Hillford, Guysborough County, Wilf Carter, known affectionately to country and western music fans as Montana Slim, lived for a time in Clementsport and attended the local school.

The *Upper Clements* Goat Island Baptist Church, so called because it faces Goat Island in the Annapolis Basin, is the oldest existing Baptist Church in Nova Scotia. The first pastor, Israel Potter, held services in this small church which is still illuminated by candles and oil lamps. Some of the original furnishings are in keeping with the authentic historical atmosphere, including a small foot pump organ with "mouse proof pedals" and two Windsor manufactured "Iron King" woodstoves.

A few miles inland from Clementsport is the community of *Clementsvale* which was once called Hessian Line Corner and its inhabitants "Hessian Liners." These ex-soldiers, eager to settle down to a peaceful farming life after the American Revolution, originally came from the German region of Hesse.

Canadian Forces Base Cornwallis, overlooking the waters of the Annapolis Basin, is located near *Deep Brook* and is the largest recruit training centre in Canada. The Base has been in operation since 1943.

St. Matthew's Anglican Church, situated in the pretty hamlet of Deep Brook, was placed on its foundations in one piece, after having been floated by barge from the neighbouring community of *Smith's Cove.*

Deep Brook resident Peter Byrne was one of the first Canadian soldiers to be treated with penicillin during World War II. After receiving serious wounds at the Battle of Ortona, Italy, in December 1943, Private Byrne was scheduled to have his badly infected leg amputated at a British hospital in Caserta. The Scottish surgeon who was to have performed the operation had visited the Annapolis Valley and had been greatly impressed by both the beauty of the land and the hospitality of the people. When he learned that Private Byrne was from the Valley, he took a special interest in his case and decided to try using penicillin, a new drug which had just arrived from England and was in very short supply. Injections of the precious drug saved young Private Byrne's leg from amputation.

Old St. Edward's Church in Clementsport, built on land purchased in 1797 from local resident Dowe Ditmars for "a peppercorn," served for more than thirty years as a landmark for ships making their way through the Digby Gut. An oil lamp lit in the church belfry served as a beacon for vessels negotiating shoreline waters.

Cornwallis Fruit Salad
(serves 4-6)

This is the type of recipe that allows you to use your imagination. The possibilities are endless. In season, you may use blueberries, strawberries, raspberries, blackberries or plums. Apricot halves, pineapple chunks, mandarin orange sections, cantaloupe balls, grapefruit sections, peeled kiwi slices or pitted large cherries are other options. Remember to have one ingredient canned as it is a super easy way to get enough juice to marinate the fruit.

1 14 oz. can peach slices in pear juice* 398 ml
1 large red apple
1 large golden apple
1 ripe pear

1 orange, peeled and seeded
½ cup grapes, red or green 125 ml
1 tsp. lemon juice 5 ml

Cut the apples and pear into bite-sized cubes — do not peel. Remove most of the membrane from the orange and chop flesh into bite-sized portions. Combine all ingredients, including the juice from the canned peaches and refrigerate to let the flavours mingle.

Serve garnished with shredded toasted coconut, raisins or honey-sweetened yogurt.

*Peaches in light syrup may also be used.

Note: You can make this salad year round, choosing from any grocery store produce section that stocks exotic as well as ordinary fruits.

Hint: Avoid using bananas as they do not keep well.

Dartmouth

AN ENTERTAINER OF RECENT YEARS, DARTMOUTHIAN Denny Doherty shot to worldwide fame as a member of the successful '60's rock group "The Mamas and the Papas."

In July, 1945, the ammunition storage depot in **Burnside** was partially destroyed by an explosion. 7,957 residents claimed property damage and were paid a total of $3,863,959.76 for reparation by the federal government.

In 1846, the Governor of Dalhousie University and prominent citizen, Dr. John MacDonald, disappeared quite literally into thin air from his home at 95 King Street in Dartmouth. No trace of foul play or any clue to his whereabouts ever surfaced and this mystery remains unsolved to this very day.

Nantucket Whalers settled in Dartmouth between 1785 and 1792. Although their stay was relatively short, the Quaker House on Ochterloney Street is a well preserved example of their lifestyle.

There is a sad story connected with the **Woodlawn** area of Dartmouth. "Babes in the Woods" is a tale of two sisters Jane and Margaret Meagher (aged six and four years) who became lost in thick forest on April 9, 1842. For seven days, 3,000 volunteers combed the woods in the Woodlawn area and were led to the girls by a dog who found the two tots, who had died from exposure, still clinging to each other. This story still stirs the hearts of all who hear it.

Dartmouth was the starting point of an ambitious project, the **Shubenacadie Canal** system, a fifty-five mile long labyrinth of lakes and man-made locks, designed to connect Halifax Harbour with the Bay of Fundy. Circumstances were such that the system was not completed, but many of the locks are still in place today.

James P. Mott, a local entrepreneur and factory owner, was involved in successful business ventures, ranging from the manufacture of soap to a chocolate factory. When he died in 1890, he was worth three-quarters of a million dollars.

The oldest continuing saltwater ferry service in Canada is the Dartmouth-to-Halifax ferry which has served the two communities since 1752.

The Dartmouth address of 26 Newcastle Street is of special interest to Maritimers because it was once the home of Dr. Helen Creighton, the well known folklorist who authored the popular *Bluenose Ghosts*.

Bluenose Mushroom Soup
(serves 4)

This soup has a creamy consistency with a definite mushroom flavour. It is a good luncheon dish or an impressive start to a complete dinner.

2 tbsp. onion, chopped *30 ml*
1 cup fresh mushrooms, sliced *250 ml*
⅓ cup celery, chopped *75 ml*
2 tbsp. butter or margarine *30 ml*

2 cups milk *500 ml*
2 tbsp. flour *25 ml*
½ tsp. salt *2 ml*
dash pepper
4 whole mushrooms

Sauté the mushrooms, onion and celery in butter until tender.

Using a blender, mix the milk, flour, salt and pepper together. Add the cooked vegetables and, using the on and off switch, blend until the vegetables are chopped finely but not puréed. The soup should have some texture to it.

Pour this mixture into a saucepan and cook over medium heat until thickened. Stir constantly and do not boil.

Remove the stems from the four whole mushrooms and chop the stems finely.

Ladle the soup into warmed bowls and garnish each serving with a whole mushroom and a sprinkling of chopped mushroom stems.

M B FP

Eskasoni

ESKASONI, DERIVED FROM THE INDIAN WORD FOR "GREEN boughs," lies on the north side of East Bay and opposite Big Pond. The first Micmac Indian to participate in the Grand Ole Opry was none other than Lee Cremo, the well known fiddler from Eskasoni.

The Poems of Rita Joe, published in 1978 by Cape Bretoner Rita Joe, reflects her desire to popularize and preserve the rich heritage of the Micmac Indians. Rita Joe's work has had the distinction of being translated into the Micmac language.

Grand Narrows, strategically located in the Barra Strait area, was in a prime position to view the mighty Hindenberg, as she made her way across Nova Scotia en route to her fatal landing in Lakehurst, New Jersey, on May 6, 1937. Folks in Grand Narrows were very excited at the approach of this awe inspiring sight. As the mighty dirigible silently floated towards the community, it seemed as if it were low enough to hit the Grand Narrows bridge. One protective resident, brandishing a shotgun, had to be restrained from shooting wildly at the airship as it passed by.

Grand Narrows Sausage Rolls
(makes 2 dozen small rolls or 8 large ones)

Homemade sausage rolls do take a bit of time to prepare but they are far superior to purchased readymade brands.

8 sausages
1 cup Cheddar cheese, finely grated *250 ml*
⅓ cup butter, softened *75 ml*
8 slices sandwich bread
2 tsp. sesame seeds *10 ml*

Fry the sausages until thoroughly cooked. Drain well on paper towels.
Beat the butter and cheese together and set aside one-third of the mixture.
Cut the crusts from the bread and roll as thin as possible with a rolling pin.
Spread all but the reserved dish of cheese mixture on one side of each slice of bread. Place a sausage on this side of the bread and roll up, pressing firmly to seal the edges. Spread the top of each roll with the reserved cheese mixture. Cut into thirds, if desired. Place, seam side down, on a lightly greased baking sheet and sprinkle with sesame seeds.
Bake at 400° F. until lightly browned for about 10-15 minutes.
Remove from the oven and serve piping hot.

Note: Sausage rolls freeze well. To serve, thaw, cut into thirds, and bake.

Glace Bay

JOEY MULLINS ESTABLISHED A WORLD INDOOR TRACK record for 600 yards in 1956, bringing honour to his home town of Glace Bay.

Daniel Petrie, a Glace Bay native, has directed such television shows as "Marcus Welby" and "The Defenders" and in 1984 filmed "The Bay Boy," the story of a young Maritimer growing up in the 1930s, in his home town of Glace Bay.

Daniel Petrie's son, Dan, wrote the box office hit "Beverly Hills Cop."

Glace Bay-born fighter Eddie Provie was christened "the Bronx Idol" by New York journalists and fans.

The first Draeger rescue equipment in North America was installed in a Glace Bay mine in 1907.

Hugh MacLennan, who has received the Governor General's award for fiction on several occasions, was born in Glace Bay in 1907. MacLennan describes himself as "a Scotsman, Presbyterian and Nova Scotian." Three of his best-loved novels are *Two Solitudes, The Watch that Ends the Night* and *Barometer Rising*.

J.B. "Kid" Adshade, at one time a Maritime Welterweight Champion, was born in Glace Bay in 1923. The "Kid" gained respect from fan and foe alike from his numerous fights in Canada and the United States.

Aptly termed the "Paris Bone Shaker," the first velocipede in Canada was ridden into Glace Bay in 1865 by Mr. Henry Poole.

"The Men of the Deeps," a choir whose members are miners, was formed in Glace Bay in 1966. This group, popular with a wide range of audiences, have travelled extensively, touching many nationalities with their stirring music.

In 1964 the first Canadian heavy water plant opened in Glace Bay, but it was not until 1976 that the first barrel of heavy water was produced.

An innovative use of waste energy in the form of hot water from the heavy water plant began in 1980. A greenhouse heated from this water produced hydroponically grown tomatoes and cucumbers in abundance.

Private John Croak of Glace Bay was posthumously awarded the Victoria Cross.

Winnie Chafe, the first woman to win the International Old Time Fiddling Contest, hails from Glace Bay.

Glace Bay Cucumber Salad
(serves 4-6)

This simple salad, with its sweet-sour taste, has a refreshing flavour, reminiscent of a mild pickle.

    1 large cucumber
    ¾ tsp. salt *3 ml*
    ¾ cup vinegar *200 ml*
    ½ cup sugar *125 ml*

Slice the cucumber very thinly (in a food processor, if possible) and sprinkle the slices with the salt. Let stand at room temperature for one hour.

Combine the vinegar and sugar in a small bowl, stirring until the sugar dissolves. Pour one-half of this mixture over the cucumber slices and stir gently. Drain thoroughly.

Just before serving, pour the remaining vinegar-sugar mixture over the cucumber slices.

Hint: To serve as a first course salad, pile a small mound of cucumber slices in a large lettuce leaf and top with several small shrimp or chunks of crab meat. Garnish with a couple of baby tomatoes. The contrast of colours, textures and tastes makes this a winning combination.

F P

Grand Pré

WHENEVER GRAND PRÉ IS MENTIONED, MOST PEOPLE think of the famous star-crossed lovers, Evangeline and Gabriel. The tragic Acadian explusion which occurred in this Acadian settlement in 1755 gave rise to many literary tributes. The Reverend Horace Conolly of Boston was unsuccessful in convincing American novelist Nathaniel Hawthorne to write a story about the tragedy, but Henry Wadsworth Longfellow, who never visited Grand Pré, penned the famous epic poem with the ringing opening phrase: "This is the forest primeval." A Canadian poet, Bliss Carman, authored the poem "Low Tide on Grand Pré in 1893.

Sir Robert Borden, prime minister of Canada between 1911 and 1920, was born in Grand Pré in 1854.

The first agricultural society in Canada was formed in Grand Pré in 1790. Taking the work ethic to heart, the society chose this motto: "Be industrious that ye may live."

Grand Pré Wines Limited was formed in 1980, a special project of political science professor, Dr. Roger Dial. The operation boasts a 500-foot long greenhouse (the longest in Nova Scotia) where vine seedlings are cultivated with tender, loving care.

The Grand Pré area is blessed with fertile farmland, much of it labouriously reclaimed from the sea. 28,455 feet of dikes, which allowed 3,000 acres of rich soil to be utilized, were constructed by the early Acadian settlers. The old dikes serve to hold back the powerful Fundy tides to this day. Made of logs packed close together with clay, the dikes are equipped with an ingenious device called an aboiteau, which is simply a wooden box with a door hinged seaward. While this door prevents sea water from entering in at high tide, it swings open at low tide and allows the land to drain itself.

The Covenanter Church at Grand Pré is the oldest existing Presbyterian Church in Nova Scotia; its first Presbyterian minister was the Reverend James Murdoch.

A blot on the historical map of Nova Scotia was the deportation of the Acadians. Of the 6,000 who were expelled in 1755, 2,000 slowly trickled back to Nova Scotia.

Grand Garlic Dip

Garlic and parsley impart a wonderful flavour to this creamy smooth dip.

1 large package cream cheese
¼ cup mayonnaise 60 ml
2 garlic cloves, crushed
¼ tsp. salt 1 ml
½ tsp. Worcestershire sauce 2 ml
dash pepper
¼ cup fresh (not dried) **parsley finely chopped** 60 ml

Cream the cheese with the other ingredients, excluding the parsley. When well combined, stir in parsley. Refrigerate.

This is a great dip for fresh vegetables. A suggested combination is whole small mushrooms, green pepper strips, carrot sticks, broccoli flowerets and "Tiny Tim" tomatoes.

Hint: Dipping is easier if the dip is allowed to come to room temperature.

FP

Halifax

HALIFAX IS CONNECTED TO ITS SISTER CITY DARTMOUTH by two bridges — the Angus L. MacDonald and the A. Murray MacKay. Early efforts at maintaining a bridge over the harbour met with failure. The first railway bridge washed out in a severe storm in 1901 while the second one simply floated away with the tide. The $11 million, mile-long Angus L. MacDonald Bridge was opened on April 2, 1955 (organizers prudently avoided an opening on April 1!). The MacDonald and MacKay bridges are insured for a total of $80 million.

The first dockyard in Canada, fittingly enough, was in Halifax and was due mainly to the efforts of a renowned explorer of western Canada, Captain Cook.

The worst day in the history of Nova Scotia's capital city fell on December 6, 1917, when two ships, one loaded with 4,000 tons of TNT, collided in Halifax Harbour. This explosion, the largest man-made one prior to Hiroshima, killed 1,630 people, injured 8,000 and left 20,000 homeless. The impact of the explosion caused a violent reaction resulting in an earthquake, tornado and tidal wave. It was followed immediately by the worst blizzard Halifax had seen in twenty years. At the time, it was estimated that $35 million worth of property was destroyed. Charitable donations, totalling $30 million, arrived from all over the world.

The Old Town Clock, erected on Citadel Hill in 1803, amazingly, did not miss a tick through the disaster in 1917. By a small miracle, the great explosion left this landmark untouched.

The first public gardens in Canada were opened in Halifax in 1753 and the first zoological gardens in North America, north of Mexico, were cultivated in *Fairview* in 1847.

The Fairview area contains the graves of 125 persons who drowned in the 1912 sinking of the Titanic in the Atlantic Ocean.

The 186-acre Point Pleasant Park in south-end Halifax has been leased to the city for 999 years for the sum of a shilling a year.

Anna Affleck, who worked in Halifax as a shop assistant, became Lady Thompson, wife of Canada's fourth prime minister. She and John Thompson travelled all the way to Portland, Maine, to be married on July 5, 1870, because John was a Methodist and Annie a Catholic and mixed marriages were not permitted in Halifax. Just after being sworn in as a member of Her Majesty's Privy Council on a visit to Britain, Thompson died unexpectedly at Windsor Castle.

Town Clock Chunky Tomato Soup
(serves 6 - 8)

In September when nature outdoes herself and neighbours drop by with baskets of ripe tomatoes, use some right away in this delicious chunky soup.

1 cup onion, chopped 250 ml
½ cup celery, chopped 125 ml
4 tbsp. butter or margarine 60 ml
6 cups tomatoes, coarsely chopped 1.5 L
3 cups chicken broth 750 ml
1 tsp. sugar 5 ml
1 tsp. salt 5 ml
¼ tsp. freshly ground black pepper 1 ml
¼ tsp. thyme 1 ml

Sauté the onions and celery in butter until tender. Add the remaining ingredients and simmer for one hour.

Serve garnished with herbed croutons:

6 slices bread, not too fresh
¼ cup butter, melted 60 ml
¼ tsp. oregano 1 ml
¼ tsp. garlic, crushed 1 ml
1½ tsp. parsley, chopped 7 ml

Cut the bread into cubes and set aside.

Add the oregano, garlic and parsley to the melted butter and sauté in a large saucepan for 2 minutes. Toss in the bread cubes and stir until coated with the seasoned butter. Spread the croutons on a baking pan and bake at 325°F. for 10 minutes. Stir and continue baking 10 minutes until the croutons are crisp. (Croutons are best cooked in a 200°F. oven and watched carefully until golden brown. The above method is for busy cooks.)

Note: The sugar added to the soup cuts the sharp acidic taste that sometimes comes from tomatoes when they are cooked.

Hint: If you prefer a thicker soup, cook it longer, allowing some of the liquid to evaporate.

FP
M (Croutons — watch carefully; do small amounts at a time.)

Kejimkujik

KEJIMKUJIK, WITH ITS SEEMINGLY UNPRONOUNCEABLE name, is one of the most beautiful parks in Canada. Its borders enclose 145 square miles of peaceful woodland, dotted with lakes and waterways. A camper's and canoeist's paradise, this area holds a fascination for biologists. Several species, unusual to Nova Scotia, thrive in Kejimkujik. The park is a natural habitat for five types of salamanders, eight kinds of frogs and toads, five species of snakes and three species of turtle. The ribbon snake and Blandings turtle, for example, are not found anywhere else in Atlantic Canada. The southern flying squirrel is unique to this particular area as well. The streams are rich in fish and the whitefish found in the lakes are highly unusual.

From the many petroglyphs drawn in the soft slate at Kejimkujik, it is obvious that this beautiful secluded area was a favourite with native peoples. One specific petroglyph, a four-legged bird surrounded by stars, is thought to be an ancient Micmac deity.

Kejimkujik Spinach Soup
(serves 4)

An excellent and elegant concoction, you will be surprised at the delicate flavour of this soup. Nutmeg is the secret ingredient here.

2 tbsp. butter or margarine *30 ml*
1 medium onion, chopped
10 oz. spinach, fresh or frozen* *300 g*
3 cups good chicken stock *750 ml* **or**
1 can chicken broth and 1½ cups water *375 ml*
¼ tsp. nutmeg *1 ml*
salt and pepper, to taste

*If using fresh spinach, remove stems and wash thoroughly. If using frozen spinach, thaw under warm running water before adding to the soup.

Sauté the onion in melted butter and cook in a large saucepan until tender. Add the spinach, chicken broth, water, nutmeg, salt and pepper. Combine well and bring to a boil.
Simmer on low heat for 2 minutes and ladle into warmed bowls.

Kentville

THE SCENIC TOWN OF KENTVILLE ON THE CORNWALLIS RIVER is located in the heart of the Annapolis Valley. Kentville takes its name from Queen Victoria's father, Prince Edward, the Duke of Kent, who visited here in 1794.

Eastern Canada's first automobile, the Mackay, was assembled in Kentville by the Nova Scotia Carriage Company in 1911. After two dozen cars were built, the Company moved to Amherst where 150 more Mackays were produced.

The Jehovah Witnesses' Kingdom Hall on Park Street in Kentville was erected by 2,000 people in less than 48 hours on September 21 and 22, 1985. The 4,200 square foot building contains a 200-seat auditorium as well as several other rooms for teaching and relaxation.

The first winery in Nova Scotia was Chipman Wines, established in Kentville in 1941 for the production of apple-based wines. Andrés Wines purchased the company in 1983.

George Warden, Abbie Warden, Ted Cumming, and Art Lightfoot, local hockey enthusiasts, established the first summer hockey school in Canada in Kentville in 1958.

An experimental horticultural station was put into operation in Kentville in 1912 and continues today as the Kentville Agricultural Centre. A memorable event takes place here each spring with the blooming of masses of varieties of rhododendrons. "Rhododendron Sunday," when the facility welcomes the public to view the colourful blooms, is a June event not to be missed.

The Cornwallis Inn, an impressive brick structure and a longtime Kentville landmark, took 208 days to erect before it opened in 1930.

In 1863 *New Ross* resident Daniel O'Neil constructed Nova Scotia's first apple barrel. He modelled it on a popular style of barrel used to store and preserve fish. For his first consignment Mr. O'Neil made 50 barrels, all by hand, hauled them nearly 50 miles with an ox team, and sold them for 50 cents per barrel. This had to be the bargain of the century!

In 1904 the first government-operated sanitorium in Canada opened its doors in Kentville. The sanitorium was a facility used for treating the once dreaded disease, tuberculosis. With the passage of time, the original eighteen-bed building expanded into a complex of twenty buildings, capable of housing four hundred patients. The Kentville "San" was considered one of the foremost and most highly respected institutions for the treatment of TB in North America.

Nearby *Camp Aldershot*, established in 1904, served as a training area for the Nova Scotia Highland Brigade, including the famed Eighty-Fifth Highland Battalion, as well as the Black Watch Regiment of Canada which had units in the Camp between 1953 and 1959.

Heart of the Valley Marinated Salad
(serves 8 - 10)

The vibrant orange and green hues in this salad are not only eye catching but the sweetness of the carrots is complemented perfectly by the onion rings and green pepper strips, which yield their flavour to the tomato-based dressing.

- 3 cups carrots, cut in thin diagonal slices 750 ml
- 2 medium onions, thinly sliced
- 1 medium green pepper, cut in thin strips
- ½ can tomato soup
- ½ cup vegetable oil 125 ml
- ½ tsp. dry mustard 2 ml
- ⅓ cup vinegar 75 ml
- ½ tsp salt 2 ml
- ¼ tsp. pepper 1 ml
- ¼ cup sugar 60 ml

Cook the carrots in boiling water for 8 minutes or until tender crisp.

Drain the carrots and run under water to cool. Place in a large bowl and add the onion rings and green pepper strips.

In a small jar combine the soup, oil, mustard, vinegar, sugar, salt and pepper. Shake well to blend and pour this marinade over the vegetables.

Stir vigorously and refrigerate for several hours or overnight.

To serve, lift the vegetables out of the dressing.

Note: This marinated carrot salad will keep five days in the refrigerator.

FP

New Glasgow

NEAR THE HEAD OF THE TIDE ON THE EAST RIVER OF PICTOU County, New Glasgow is the home of Carrie Best, who started the first Nova Scotian newspaper for blacks. The "Clarion" commenced circulation in 1946. Best, who gained a reputation as a columnist, editor, radio commentator and human rights organizer, was awarded the Order of Canada in 1974.

At the turn of the century, New Glasgow was a booming ship building centre. The "Richard Smith," the first Nova Scotian steamship, was built here and the "James William," the only steel sailing vessel constructed in Canada, was launched in New Glasgow in 1908.

New Glasgow native George Frederick Cameron (1854-1885) devoted his short life to poetry composition and is considered by modern literary critics to be an accomplished rhetorical poet. Never published during his lifetime, a volume of rather sombre poetry entitled *Lyrics on Freedome, Love and Death* was printed posthumously.

When twenty pairs of English sparrows were set free from their cages in New Glasgow in 1874, it marked the first recorded importation of this type of bird into Canada.

Nearby **Trenton**, named after a town of the same name in New Jersey, was the location William Godkin Beach chose to establish the Nova Scotia Glass Company in 1881. Although it operated for only eleven years, it produced some fine examples of Canadian pressed glass, including such collectors' patterns as Queen Victoria, Grape and Vine, and Crown or Pillar.

Jodi MacCuish found a very intriguing creature in Trenton in 1985. Biologists claim her eight-legged frog was a one-in-a-million freak of nature.

Trenton, the "Birthplace of Steel," is recognized for its steelworks, including the Hawker Siddeley Canada Limited plant which has the largest forging press in Canada.

New Glasgow native Donald E. Smith held the longest term for a Scouting officer in the province of Nova Scotia — thirty-seven years.

New Glasgow Marinated Cole Slaw
(serves 8 - 10)

In years past, when folks depended on root cellars and cold storage rooms, cabbage was about the only green vegetable available for salads throughout the winter. There are endless numbers of recipes for cole slaws with different dressings. This version has a sweet flavour, enhanced by the muted tang of cider vinegar. Served as a side dish, cole slaw does marvellous things to sandwiches, hamburgers, barbeques and salad plates.

1 cup vegetable oil *250 ml*
¾ cup sugar *200 ml*
¾ cup cider vinegar *200 ml*
1 medium cabbage, shredded
2 medium carrots, grated
1 medium onion, grated
1 green pepper, seeded and chopped
1 tbsp. dry mustard, sifted *15 ml*
1½ tsp. celery seed *7 ml*
¾ tsp. salt *3 ml*

Combine the oil, sugar and vinegar in a medium saucepan and bring to a boil.

Meanwhile, combine the cabbage, carrot, onion and green pepper in a large bowl. Sprinkle this mixture with mustard, celery seed and salt and toss to blend well.

Pour the hot oil over the cabbage and mix well. Allow to chill for at least 24 hours before using.

To serve, lift the cole slaw out of the dressing with a slotted spoon.

Note: This cole slaw can be refrigerated for two weeks.

Hint: To take the work out of this recipe, use a blender or a food processor for shredding and grating.

B FP

Port Morien

THE FIRST COAL MINING OPERATION IN CANADA BEGAN here in 1920.

In 1908 William Glover organized the first Canadian Boy Scout troop in Port Morien.

Table Head and Port Morien were locations for pioneer work in the field of trans-Atlantic wireless messages. Marconi succeeded on December 15, 1902, in transmitting from Table Head to Poldhu, Cornwall, the first trans-Atlantic wireless message. Written by the London Times correspondent in Cape Breton, the message conveyed greetings to England and Italy. This marked the first time a trans-Atlantic communication originated in North America. The first transoceanic wireless operator was an American named Leonard Johnstone.

In March 1903, Table Head, Poldhu, and the London Times introduced the first trans-Atlantic news service, called the Marconigram. 1903 also saw the first transmission of messages to a ship, the "Lacania", crossing the Atlantic. This ship-to-shore communication is still vital to ships today.

In 1904 the Table Head operation was moved to Port Morien where four times the volume of messages were generated. Clifden, Ireland, became the reception station for Port Morien transmissions, with the first transoceanic public messages making their way to the "Old Country" on October 17, 1907.

Port Morien Mussel Kabobs
(serves 4)

Deceptively simple to prepare, this mussel recipe provides a delicious and light beginning to a meal. Shish kabobs are always a bit exotic, and the garnish of lemon, parsley, and mushroom sets each plate off to perfection.

2-3 lb. mussels, scrubbed clean *1.5 kg*
5 slices Black Forest ham*
¼ cup butter, melted *60 ml*
mushrooms, lemon, parsley for garnish

*(do not substitute sweet ham)

Steam the mussels in a small amount of boiling water. Discard any shells that have not opened. Remove the mussels from their shells, checking carefully for any bits of shell or small pebbles. Set aside.

Divide each slice of ham into one-inch wide strips. Wrap each strip around 2 mussels. Slide the packet onto a small wooden skewer. Each skewer should hold 5-6 rolls.

Brush the kabobs generously with melted butter and place in a hot oven. Cook until steaming hot. (These may be microwaved in a couple of minutes on high heat.)

Place a skewer on a small serving plate and garnish with a sliced mushroom spread out in a fan shape, a slice of lemon and a sprig of parsley.

Note: If you don't have the small disposable wooden skewers, fasten each little mussel bundle with a toothpick and serve several on each plate with a tiny dish of hot dipping butter, if you wish.

M

Sable Island

IT IS CLAIMED THAT THERE HAS BEEN AT LEAST ONE SHIPWRECK for each of the 4,625 miles of Nova Scotia's coastline. Sable Island, southeast of Halifax, at the red-letter nautical position of 43°57' N and 59°55' W, can certainly claim a giant's share of these sea disasters. Aptly called the "Graveyard of the Atlantic," Sable Island has a grim reputation with mariners, considering that an estimated 200 wrecked ships haunt its treacherous sand bars. Twenty miles long and one mile wide, Sable Island is composed totally of sand — there are no rocks or trees and the landscape is endlessly shifting and reshaping itself.

Sable Island came into prominence in 1971 when an offshore oil discovery was made nearby.

The history of Sable Island goes back as far as 1518 when Baron de Tery landed the first domesticated cattle to arrive in Canada. The first recorded gardens in Nova Scotia were planted here in 1548. Marquis de la Roche, who brought fifty-two settlers to the little island in 1598, named it Bourbon.

At one time Sable Island was famous for its ponies, and although they have virtually disappeared, the Island is still roamed by wild horses.

Hundreds of species of birds and seals frequent Sable Island; in fact, it is the only known breeding ground of the Ipswich sparrow. This breeding range is the smallest one of any bird in Canada.

The first recorded shipwreck off Sable Island occurred in 1583 when the "Admiral" foundered there. A more recent naval disaster happened in 1981 when the "Euro Princess", a Norwegian grain carrier ran aground during a vicious storm. Braving ferocious gales and waters, the crew of two Canadian Armed Forces helicopters managed to rescue all twenty-six "Euro Princess" crew members airlifting them one by one off the sinking vessel.

Sable Island Shrimp Pâté
(makes four small crocks)

In this unique pâté, the intense flavour of shrimp is offset nicely by the garlic and thyme and tempered by the sweetness of the butter.

1 lb. tiny shrimp, cooked *450 g*
or
3-4 cans shrimp, drained, rinsed and drained again
1 cup butter *250 ml*
1 clove garlic, minced
¼ tsp. thyme *1 ml*
pepper to taste

Melt the butter in a saucepan and add the shrimp, garlic, thyme and pepper. Stirring gently, simmer a few moments until heated through.
Remove from the stove and spoon into a blender (or food processor) in two batches. Purée until smooth.
Stir the two batches together until somewhat cooled.
Pack in little crocks and cover tightly with plastic wrap. Refrigerate.
Bring to room temperature before serving and garnish with fresh, chopped parsley, if desired.

Note: This pâté freezes extremely well and adds a festive touch to any occasion when it is served.

B FP F

Sheet Harbour

THIS HALIFAX COUNTY TOWN IS ONE OF THE PRETTIEST IN Nova Scotia and views of the Atlantic Ocean from the town and surrounding area are varied and beautiful.

Dr. Finlay MacMillan, a graduate of the first class of Dalhousie Medical School in 1872, practised medicine in Sheet Harbour for fifty years. On his 80th birthday, he emerged temporarily from retirement, when the local doctor was away, to deliver a healthy set of twins.

Nearby *Tangier* has become internationally known for its delicious smoked fish. It is said the best smoked salmon in the world is produced by J. Willy Krauch and Sons Limited of Tangier.

The Indian name for Tangier, "Wospegeak," means the sunshine is reflected from the water" and certainly describes the physical attractions of the shoreline.

When drinking from a clear pool of water in Tangier in 1860, a man discovered a gold nugget the size of a buckshot. During the thirty years of gold mining in this area, more than 26,000 ounces of the precious metal were extracted.

The Halifax County community of **Moose River** held the nation spellbound during the continuous, live radio coverage of the Moose River Mine Disaster in April 1936. This event marked a first in the history of Canadian media as the Moose River Mine Disaster was the first such disaster in North America to be covered by continuous on-the-spot radio news broadcasts. It is estimated that an audience of 100 million people tuned in to the broadcasts. Three Toronto men, Dr. D. Edwin Robertson, Alfred Scadding and Herman Magill, who were inspecting the Moose River Mine, were trapped by a cave-in. Although Magill died, Robertson and Scadding survived 240 hours in the shaft. A cairn was erected here in honour of the brave crew from Stellarton who risked their own lives to save the disaster victims.

Charles Wood, a native Haligonian, was the first Canadian to be killed in the Boer War of 1897. To honour him, **Chaswood** was so christened by an act of the Provincial Legislature in 1901. An interesting historical footnote is that Charles Wood was the son of John Taylor, a one-time captain of the Tallahassee, the fastest ship in the Confederate navy. Charles Wood was also the grandson of General Zachary Taylor, one-time President of the United States

East River was the site of the first sulphite mill in Canada; it commenced operation here in 1885.

Tangier Smoked Salmon Bites
(about 2 dozen appetizers)

A quick and simple appetizer to prepare, the elegant simplicity of the smoked salmon offsets the bland taste and smooth-textured cream cheese perfectly.

¼ **lb. smoked salmon, very thinly sliced** *115 g*
¼ **cup cream cheese, softened** *60 ml*
6 slices fresh dark rye bread
fresh parsley or dill

Remove the crusts from the bread and spread with cream cheese, being careful to coat the bread to the very edge.
Cut each slice of bread into four fingers. Cut strips of smoked salmon and lay on top of each bread finger.
Arrange on a platter, generously garnished with sprigs of parsley or dill. Cover tightly with plastic wrap and refrigerate till served.
NOTE: Butter can be used instead of cream cheese.

Stellarton

NAMED STELLARTON IN 1870 AFTER THE "STELLA" COAL variety found in abundance here, this Pictou County town was Canada's pioneer coal mining centre. In fact, the 48-foot-thick Ford seam is reputed to be the widest in the world.

Stellarton was the birthplace of the co-operatives idea with the first "co-op" being established here in 1861. The concept of co-operatives and credit unions has proven to be highly successful and each new one that springs up is patterned after the Stellarton prototype.

Private James Peter Robertson, of nearby Albion Mines, was posthumously awarded the Victoria Cross for the exceptional courage and valour he exhibited in the heat of the fray at the Battle of Passchendaele in World War I.

The Sobey family of Stellarton turned a one-store family operation into the largest grocery store chain in Atlantic Canada. One of its widely known members was honoured in 1975 as Canada's Businessman of the Year. His exploits and the Sobey empire have been examined in Harry Bruce's recent book, *Frank Sobey: The Man and the Empire*.

The "Samson," the first coal-burning locomotive to travel on iron rails, began work in Stellarton in 1839.

Born in neighbouring Albion Mines in 1835, George Munro Grant was a great naturalist and explorer. He travelled with Sir Sandford Fleming across Canada to map out a route for a transcontinental railway. His book *Ocean to Ocean* won him widespread recognition in 1873. He served as Principal of Queen's University in Kingston, Ontario, for twenty-five years.

When Stellarton minister, Reverend Morris Taylor inherited $500 at the turn of the century, he used it to build a church in **Bridgeville**. When population there dropped, the building was dismantled and transported by rail to **Windsor Junction** where it remains today as St. Stephen's Church.

Special Stellarton Stuffed Mushrooms
(serves 6)

Stuffed mushrooms are a particular favourite of my husband who enjoys them served before dinner or as an extra treat with barbequed steak, roast beef or a fancy chicken breast dish. These attractive hot little treats — succulent mushroom caps with their spicy fillings and pungent cheese dustings — are well worth the extra effort to prepare them.

24 large mushrooms
2 tbsp. butter or margarine *30 ml*
2 tbsp. green onion, minced *30 ml*
2 tbsp. fresh parsley, chopped *30 ml*
4 crackers, finely crushed

2 tsp. sherry *10 ml*
2 tsp. HP or A-1 sauce *10 ml*
¼ tsp. thyme, crushed *1 ml*
1 tsp. soy sauce *5 ml*
4 tsp. Parmesan cheese, grated *20 ml*

Choose large, well-shaped mushrooms and clean them gently with a damp cloth or rinse them quickly under cold, running water and dry immediately. Snap out the stems and chop them finely. Melt the butter in a small frypan and sauté the chopped stems, onion and parsley for a few moments. Stir in the sherry, cracker crumbs, HP or A-1 sauce, thyme, and soy sauce.

Place the mushroom caps, top down, on an ungreased baking pan. Divide the stuffing mixture among the 2 dozen mushrooms, placing a small amount in each one. Finally, sift a bit of Parmesan cheese on each mushroom cap.

At this point, you can refrigerate until ready for baking.

Bake at 375°F. for 7 - 10 minutes or until piping hot.

Hint: When cooked in a microwave stuffed mushroom caps retain their firm texture beautifully due to no loss of moisture.

M

Yarmouth

CHAMPLAIN CALLED THIS AREA PORT FORCHU OR FORKED Harbour. Strategically located at the western end of the province, Yarmouth is linked to the United States by the "Bluenose" ferry which began its regular trips to Bar Harbour, Maine, in 1956.

In 1897 a "runic" stone was found in the Yarmouth area. Historians and archeologists have speculated on its significance as evidence of a visit by Norsemen here as early as the year 1000.

A Yarmouth native, Captain John Patch, is credited with inventing the screw propellor, a revolutionary feature still employed on ocean-going vessels today. Unfortunately, Captain Patch was not recognized for his contribution to marine engineering during his lifetime.

Yarmouth born Jean Eldridge Marshall has been singing since she was two years old. Her career has taken her all over the world, performing in evangelical tours of South America and Asia. She has also had the opportunity of singing before the Queen Mother and Prime Minister Diefenbaker and performing on "the Don Messer Show" and in the Kipawo Theatre production of "The Sound of Music."

Yarmouth was the birthplace of the financial wizard Isaak Walton Killam. Sometimes called the richest man in Canada, his secretive nature earned him the title of "the mystery man of Canada." His dying wish was that his accumulated wealth find its way back to Nova Scotia; as a result, his widow donated $8 million to the Isaak Walton Killam Children's Hospital in Halifax as well as $30 million to Dalhousie University, which is thought to be the largest single gift ever bestowed on a Canadian university.

Labeled the "King of Pain," the time honoured home remedy Minard's Liniment was manufactured in Yarmouth for fifty years. Developed by Nova Scotian Dr. Levi Minard in 1886, the liniment has been produced in central Canada since 1967 and is still "good for man or beast."

Yarmouth's Mountain Cemetery boasts the first mortuary chapel in Canada and the first monument erected by the Nova Scotian Government to honour a Nova Scotian, Hubert Huntington, for his service to the government between 1830 and 1850.

A beautiful and unique sight a few miles northwest of Yarmouth is "Lupine Hill" in full bloom in early summer. Lupines were brought to the Yarmouth area in 1849 from California and, in spite of the harsh climate, have flourished.

Cape Forchu lighthouse, located high on a windswept rock cliff, has been in operation since 1840. Equipped with mercury vapour bulbs, the lights are visible for thirty miles. Countless ships and small fishing craft rely on this light to guide them safely through Yarmouth harbour.

Born in Yarmouth in 1920, Nelson Surette has had a varied career, having worked as an upholsterer, interior decorator, sailmaker, carpenter, landscaper and gravedigger. Yet his greatest talent lies in his artistic ability. His painted figures are larger than life and his interpretation of his subjects is entirely sympathetic, endowing the humblest of occupations with a dignity and inner goodness. One of his well-known pictures is simply called, "Clamdiggers."

Bowman Law of Yarmouth was elected in 1902 to the House of Commons. He served as the local Member of Parliament until his death in 1916, when he perished in the fire that swept through the Parliament Buildings in February of that year. There is a plaque in memory of Bowman B. Law in the new Parliament Buildings in Ottawa.

The Best Yarmouth Seafood Chowder
(serves 8 - 10)

I clipped this recipe from an Ottawa newspaper several years ago. The lady who submitted it was Mrs. Gerald Regan, wife of the Premier of Nova Scotia from 1970 to 1978. It has been tested on friends from all over Canada who agree it is worth its weight in gold. Not only is it an excellent meal, it is also a marvellous showcase for Nova Scotia's unbeatable seafood products.

1½ cups potatoes, diced *375 ml*
¾ cup onion, chopped *200 ml*
⅓ cup celery, diced *75 ml*
½ tsp. salt *2 ml*
½ lb. scallops *225 g*
½ lb. haddock, deboned *225 g*
½ lb. halibut *225 g*

1 can lobster paste
½-1 lb. cooked lobster meat *225-450 g*
¼ lb. shrimp *125 g*
2 cans evaporated milk
2 cups milk *500 ml*
¼ cup butter *60 ml*
2 tbsp. sherry *25 ml*
salt and pepper to taste

Cover the potatoes, onion, celery and ½ tsp. (2 ml) salt with hot water and simmer for 20 minutes until fork tender.

At the same time, steam the scallops, haddock and halibut until the fish flakes. Drain the vegetables and combine with the fish. Set aside. Heat the milk in a large pot and gently stir in the vegetables, fish, lobster paste, lobster meat, shrimp and butter. Heat gently, being careful not to bring to a boil. Add salt and pepper and stir in the sherry. Ladle into warmed bowls and serve immediately with hot rolls.

Note: You should be especially careful when cooking milk or cream-based soups; they will sometimes curdle if brought to a boil. Although this does not really affect the taste, it is decidedly unappealing to the eye.

ACCOMPANIMENTS

Bear River

PERCHED ALONG THE STEEP BANKS OF THE BEAR RIVER AND nestled in a cluster of hills, this picturesque village has been aptly described as "the Switzerland of Nova Scotia."

Major William Morris Jones (1895-1969), a native of Bear River, was the first Allied officer to parachute into Yugoslavia to organize guerilla warfare against the Germans. Referred to as the "Lawrence of Yugoslavia," the Germans found Major Jones so troublesome that they offered 10,000 gold marks for him, dead or alive.

The Bear River, which runs through the centre of the village, takes its name from one of two early explorers, either Simon Imbert, a relief ship commander to Port Royal in 1612, or Louis Hebert, the first North American apothecary, who arrived with Champlain in 1604. When Hebert died his widow, Marie Hubou, became Canada's first nurse. A commemorative stamp was issued in 1985 to honour this early pioneer.

Bear River gained some measure of notoriety at the turn of the century for the sensational murder of teenager Annie Kempton. She was brutally slain by a young man named Wheeler who was tried, convicted and hanged in the early morning hours, depriving the curious of the spectacle. Annie Kempton's tombstone can be seen in Bear River's Mount Hope Cemetery and bears this inscription:

> Erected to the memory of Annie Kempton, aged 15 years who lost her life January 27, 1896, in her father's house in a desperate struggle to preserve her honour.

Reverend Dr. Thomas B. MacDormand, a writer and theologian, was born in Bear River in 1904. Among the books he has written, the *Judson Concordance to Hymns* (1959) is the only such concordance in the world. A man of many accomplishments, Rev. MacDormand has preached as far away as Russia and has received five honorary degrees.

Bear River has produced a number of avid sportsmen. Watson Peck has gained national recognition as a woodsman, guide, canoeist, and tilter. Eber Peck has been a well known logrolling champion, as has Viola Paul, one of the first women to get involved in the sport.

Bear River Cherry Blossom Loaf
(makes 2 small loaves or one large loaf)

The Bear River Cherry Carnival is an annual event and although this cherry bread uses preserved cherries, it is often served as a tasty treat, in keeping with the holiday theme. Its unusual colour comes from the pink of the cherry syrup and the fragrance of the bread brings to mind beautiful cherry trees with their boughs laden with delicate clusters of blossoms.

¼ **cup shortening** 60 ml
1 **cup brown sugar** 250 ml
1 **egg, beaten**
2 **cups flour** 500 ml
½ **tsp. salt** 2 ml

2 **tsp. baking powder** 10 ml
⅔ **cup milk** 175 ml
⅓ **cup cherry syrup** 75 ml
½ **cup maraschino cherries, quartered** 125 ml
½ **cup walnuts, chopped** 125 ml

Cream the shortening and sugar together, add the egg and beat well.

Sift the flour, salt and baking powder together and set aside.

Combine the milk and cherry syrup and add to the shortening mixture alternately with the flour mixture. Fold in the cherries and walnuts and spoon into greased pans.

Baked in a preheated 350° F. oven about 45 minutes or until the cake tester comes clean.

Note: I make two loaves with this recipe instead of the larger single loaf. It is always useful to have an extra individually wrapped sweetbread loaf waiting in the freezer to be given as a gift to some deserving friend.

F

Berwick

ORIGINALLY NAMED "CONDON'S CORNER," THIS KINGS County community was renamed after the English town on the Tweed; however, whereas the British pronounce it "Ber-ick," the Nova Scotian version is "Ber-wick."

One of the first two jacketed vegetable storage depots in Canada was constructed at Ron Sawler's farm in Berwick in 1968. The other was built in *Waterville* and was operated by the Cornwallis Fruit Company.

Two very well known Maritime food supply companies began their operations in Berwick — the Berwick Bakery (1924) and H.D. Larsen meat packers (1947).

The nationally known baritone, Earle Spicer, was born in Berwick in 1891. Before his death in 1969, Spicer had the distinction of performing at Buckingham Palace, the White House and Rideau Hall.

St. Mary's Church, in nearby *Auburn*, was built in 1790 and is interesting from an historical point of view for many reasons, the most unique one being that its walls are plastered with powdered mussel shells gathered from the seashore at Morden.

Called "Kobetek," a word meaning "beaver's home," by the Indians, *Aylesford* takes its present name from the fourth Earl of Aylesford, Lord of the Bedchamber to King George III. Aylesford is renowned for its great stretches of peat bogs.

Berwick Potato Flan
(4 servings)

This is an easy, dressed up potato dish. Don't be put off by dehydrated onion flakes. They brown delicately on top and impart a sweet, crunchy taste to the potatoes, quite different from that fresh onions would produce.

4 medium potatos, peeled and rinsed
garlic salt
paprika
⅔ cup dehydrated onion flakes *175 ml*
4 tbsp. oil *60 ml*
parsley, for garnish

Slice the potatoes thinly and evenly. Pat dry with paper towel.

Spread one-half of the potatoes evenly over the bottom of a large, shallow baking dish with a cover.

Sprinkle with garlic salt, paprika and one-half of the onion flakes. Repeat this procedure with a second potato, onion flake layer and pour the oil over the top. Cover and cook at 400°F. for about 30 minutes or until the potatoes are tender. Garnish with chopped parsley or a sprinkling of dried parsley flakes.

FP

Canso

ONE THEORY IS THAT THE NAME OF THIS GUYSBOROUGH County town was derived from "ganso," the Spanish word for goose, due to the large flocks of wild geese which frequent the area each spring. Another idea is that the Indian word "kamsok," meaning "opposite lofty cliffs," may have been corrupted to Canso.

The Canso area has the distinction of being home to the first Baptist Women's Missionary Aid Society in the world. It was set up here in 1870. Thirty-five years earlier, religious feelings were also running high in Canso when rioting Irish Catholics and Protestant Orangemen disrupted the normal activities of the town.

The multi-talented Constance Tomkinson, who was born in Canso in 1915, turned her hand to acting, dancing and writing and found time to perform in the show team entertaining World War II troops.

In 1873, a great storm blowing in off the North Atlantic demolished stores, wharves, ships, and the *Crow Harbour* Baptist Church. The Catholic Church was lifted entirely off its foundations by ferocious gales.

Across Chedabucto Bay from the town of Canso and spanning the Strait of Canso lies the Canso Causeway linking Cape Breton Island with mainland Nova Scotia. When it opened in 1955, the Canso Causeway was the deepest in the world. In fact, the concrete used to construct it could make a sidewalk four feet wide and four inches thick, stretching from Sydney to Halifax. The rock filling in the roadway would be more than enough to rebuild the famous Egyptian pyramid of Cheops. Harry MacKenzie drove the first car across the Canso Causeway on December 11, 1954.

Canso Cloud Biscuits
(makes 10 - 12 biscuits)

Light and airy, these biscuits are scrumptious served hot from the oven with whipped cream cheese, preserves or sweet butter. They add that special homemade touch to a family gathering, a cosy afternoon tea or an elegant ladies' luncheon.

2 cups flour 500 ml
1 tbsp. sugar 15 ml
4 tsp. baking powder 20 ml
½ tsp. salt 2 ml

½ cup shortening 125 ml
1 egg, beaten
⅔ cup milk 175 ml

Preheat oven to 450° F.

Combine the flour, sugar, baking powder, salt and shortening.

Add the beaten egg and milk to the flour mixture and stir well. Knead about 20 times. Roll onto a floured surface and cut into biscuit rounds, making them fairly thick, at least 1 inch (2.5 cm).

Place on an ungreased baking sheet and bake for 10 - 12 minutes.

F

Cheticamp

THE NAME OF THIS INVERNESS COUNTY COMMUNITY HAS become synonymous with Cheticamp hooked mats and rugs, a traditional Cape Breton art form for many years. These beautifully crafted rugs are popular with visitors from afar as well as Maritimers. Probably the best known craftsperson from this area is Elizabeth Lefort, whose tapestries decorate the walls of the White House, Buckingham Palace, the Vatican and the National Museum of Man in Ottawa. Elizabeth Lefort can hook precisely fifty-five stitches a minute!

Another Inverness County community once known as Broad Cove March was renamed **Dunvegan** after a castle in Skye, a Hebridean Island off the coast of Scotland, reflecting the rich Scottish background of the Cape Bretoners in this area.

A well-known Nova Scotian politician, the Honourable Angus L. MacDonald, was born in Dunvegan in 1890. He served as premier of the province from 1933 to 1940 and from 1945 to 1954, dying in office in 1954. The Angus L. MacDonald Bridge, connecting Halifax to her sister city of Dartmouth, is a lasting memorial to this outstanding Nova Scotian.

Moses Coady, author of *Masters of their Own Destiny* (1939), was born in **Northeast Margaree**. He was recognized as a world authority on rural problems and received the American Carnegie award for work in this field. He was also involved with the cooperative movement and the formation of the world famous Coady Institute in Antigonish.

Angus Chisholm, a self-taught fiddler who made his home in **Margaree Forks**, was one of Nova Scotia's first musicians to make a 78 rpm recording.

Dunvegan Barley Casserole
(serves 4 - 6)

This is an excellent casserole to serve with game, turkey, lamb or beef. The barley takes on a nutty flavour which is enhanced by buttery mushrooms and onions. It also freezes well, if you wish to prepare it ahead of time.

> 1 cup *pearl* barley 250 ml
> 1 large onion, chopped
> ½ lb. mushrooms, sliced 250 g
> ¼ cup butter or margarine 60 ml
> 2 cups beef broth (or chicken stock) 250 ml
> salt and pepper to taste

Melt the butter in a saucepan. Sauté the onions and mushrooms in the butter until softened. Add the barley and, stirring frequently, brown it lightly.

Butter a large casserole dish. Pour the barley and vegetable mixture into the casserole dish and sprinkle with salt and pepper.

Pour one cup of the beef broth over the barley mixture. Cover and bake at 350° F. for 30 minutes.

Uncover and add the second cup of broth. Continue baking until the liquid is absorbed and the barley is tender.

Hint: For a variation on the theme, sprinkle the top of the casserole with ½ cup (125 ml) toasted slivered almonds when the second cup of liquid is added. (Omit the mushrooms and onion.) Try an herbed version, again omitting the onions and mushrooms and substituting ¼ cup (60 ml) finely chopped green onion, ½ cup (125 ml) finely chopped celery and ½ cup (125 ml) finely chopped parsley. Sauté these ingredients with the barley in the melted butter.

F

Halifax

THE LITTLE DUTCH CHURCH ON BRUNSWICK STREET, WHICH measures forty feet by twenty feet, sheltered the first Lutheran congregation in Canada in 1758. Its graveyard contains a most interesting tombstone with the following inscription:

> In memory of Resteller Jane A. Ratsey, Foster Sister of Her Royal Highness, the Princess Royal of England and daughter of Mr. R. Ratsey of H.M. Royal Naval Yard. Died of malignant scarlet fever, March 1st, 1841, aged 3 years 4 months and 15 days.

Our Lady of Sorrows Church in Holy Cross Cemetery was built by 2,000 people on August 31, 1843.

St. Paul's, called the "Westminster Abbey of Canada," is situated in the heart of downtown Halifax overlooking the Parade Square. The first Protestant church in Canada, St. Paul's also held the first Sunday School services in Canada. It was here in April 1769 that the first oratorio was sung in Canada. The first broadcast of a church service in Halifax took place here in September 1926 with the first telecast of a church service in the Maritime Provinces taking place on Christmas Eve 1955. In March 1965, the first folk service conducted in Canada drew large crowds of young people.

St. Paul's has seen more than 12,000 weddings and 20,000 burials and has received seven million worshippers over the years. It has the only English Church Register in Canada kept under the old Julian Calendar.

St. Paul's Church is a "Church of the Royal Foundation," one of two such churches in Canada, the other being the Mohawk Chapel in Brantford, Ontario.

The Right Reverend Charles Inglis (1787-1816), the first Bishop in Canada, at one time had jurisdiction over a diocese stretching from Newfoundland to Detroit. The Bishop is buried in St. Paul's Church.

St. Mary's Basilica on the corner of Spring Garden Road and Barrington Street, has the tallest polished granite spire in the world — it soars 189 feet above the sidewalk.

St. Matthew's United Church on Barrington Street was built in 1858, its first minister being the Reverend Aaron Cleveland who was the great, great grandfather of American president Grover Cleveland.

The first Protestant missionary from Canada, a Baptist lady named Minnie DeWolfe, set out from Halifax to go to Burmah in 1867.

St. George's Round Church on the corner of Brunswick Street and Cornwallis Street is the third oldest church in Halifax and the first round church in North America. St. George's was honoured in 1983 with a royal visit by Charles and Diana, Prince and Princess of Wales. The interesting weather vane perched atop the church tower was raised in 1835 to commemorate the passing of Halley's Comet. The basement of St. George's Church contains the grave of Joseph Frederick Wallet Des Barres, first Lieutenant Governor of Cape Breton.

A talented artist, Des Barres was instrumental in charting Nova Scotia's coastline and in sketching the vessels plying the coastal waters at that

Halifax Hovis Bread

This nutritious bread, which you can make in a jiffy, has the taste and look of a yeast-based whole wheat loaf. It is wonderful with homebaked beans — the traditional Saturday night dinner in Nova Scotia.

1½ cups white flour 375 ml
1½ cups whole wheat flour 375 ml
2½ tsp. baking powder 12 ml
½ tsp. baking soda 2 ml
½ tsp. salt 2 ml
3 tbsp. brown sugar 45 ml
1¾ cups milk 425 ml

Simply mix all of the ingredients together until thoroughly combined and pour into a well-greased loaf pan.
Bake one hour at 350° F.
Allow to cool for a short time after removing from the oven but serve while still warm.

F

Town Crier Turnip Puff
(serves 8 - 10)

This fluffy vegetable dish dresses up a rather low profile vegetable — the good old turnip. It is a delicious accompaniment to pork or turkey.

5 cups turnip (1 medium size) 1.25 L
1 cup applesauce 250 ml
2 tbsp. butter 30 ml
2 eggs, beaten
1 tbsp. brown sugar 15 ml

3 tbsp. flour 45 ml
1 tsp. baking powder 5 ml
¾ tsp. salt 3 ml
⅛ tsp. pepper .5 ml

Cook the turnip in boiling water until tender. Mash well.
Stir the butter into the hot turnip until the butter is completely melted.
Combine the applesauce with the beaten eggs and sugar. Mix the flour, baking powder, salt and pepper together and add all at once to the applesauce mixture. Stir until combined.
Combine the applesauce mixture with the mashed turnip and pour into a greased casserole dish. Chill for 45 minutes and then bake in a 350° F. oven for 35 minutes.

F (unbaked)

time. A collection of his work entitled *Atlantic Neptune*, is a showcase for his surveying and artistic abilities. A strong and determined man with a hearty zest for life, he lived to be 103 years old.

The specially reserved Lieutenant Governor's pew in St. Matthew's United Church is decorated with part of the carpet that was used in Westminster Abbey for the Coronation of Queen Elizabeth II.

The oldest tombstone in St. Paul's cemetery is a marker for Mrs. Martha Parker who died on May 28, 1752.

THE FIRST COVERED SKATING RINK IN NORTH AMERICA WAS enjoyed by Halifax residents in 1863.

George Dixon of Halifax who, at the age of twenty-four, won the world featherweight title, became the first Canadian to win such a world title.

Ice hockey, or "hurley," was first played in Halifax 1825.

The International Town Criers Championships are held in Halifax each summer when Historic Properties on the waterfront comes alive with the ringing of the competitors' voices.

The first yacht club in Canada was organized on the scenic Northwest Arm in 1837. The Royal Nova Scotia Yacht Squadron slips are still crowded with various types of sailing boats today.

Haligonian Nancy Garapick broke the 200-yard backstroke record on April 27, 1975, and followed it up with two bronze medals in the 1976 Olympics.

In 1985 swimmer Susan Mason (MacLeod), at twenty-five years of age, became the youngest person ever elected to the Nova Scotia Sports Hall of Fame. In 1976 she set sixty-two provincial senior and age-group records. At the 1976 National Championships her time in the 1,500 metre freestyle was sixteen seconds faster than the provincial men's record!

The Royal Nova Scotia Yacht Squadron hosts the highly competitive yacht race which takes place every other year between Marblehead, Massachusetts and **Chebucto Head**. The first 360-mile race took place in August 1939 and, with the exception of the war years of 1940-46, the Marblehead Race has been a regular and popular event.

The Dalplex dome, when built in the early 1980's, was the only one of its kind in the world. It is an air-supported, thin membrane of stainless steel, especially designed to give the building a low profile, which would be pleasing to the eye and in keeping with the beautiful residential area of south-end Halifax.

IN OPERATION (SO TO SPEAK!) SINCE THE 1850's, HALIFAX'S Victoria General Hospital is the oldest continuously functioning hospital in the Maritimes. Described as an acute tertiary care hospital, the V.G. serves all of Nova Scotia as well as the other Maritime Provinces on a limited basis. This hospital makes more use of x-rays than any other hospital in Canada. Ranked as one of the top ten Canadian hospitals, the Victoria General has one of the highest volumes of open heart surgery operations. The only centre east of Montreal for kidney transplants, more are performed

Maverick Great Brussels Sprouts
(serves 4-6)

Even if you are not very fond of brussels sprouts, you will probably enjoy this dish. The secret is to serve it while the brussel sprouts are piping hot.

4 cups brussels sprouts, cleaned *1 L*
1 onion, finely chopped
2 slices bacon, chopped
2 tbsp. butter *30 ml*
salt and pepper to taste
dash nutmeg

Place the sprouts in boiling water and cook until fork tender. Plunge into ice water and drain well.
Meanwhile, sauté the onion and bacon in the melted butter. Add the sprouts and season with salt and pepper. Sprinkle with the nutmeg. Sauté, stirring frequently until the sprouts are heated through.
Serve immediately.

Hint: To retain the brilliant green of these little vegetables, the ice water bath is essential.

Dingle Dumplings
(serves 6)

When my grandmother Sarah Kerr left Ireland with her husband and five children in 1927 to start a new life in Nova Scotia, this was one of her favourite recipes; my mother also made great use of it. She served these fluffy "dough boys" in stews, on cooked fruit and with soups.

2 cups flour *500 ml*
4 tsp. baking powder *20 ml*
½ tsp. salt *2 ml*
3 tbsp. shortening *45 ml*
1 cup milk *250 ml*

Combine the flour, baking powder and salt. Cut in the shortening with a pastry cutter or two knives. Add the milk and stir until combined.
To cook, add the dumplings to a pot containing enough liquid to steam the dough and cover with a tightly-fitting lid.

Hint: If you wish to fancy up the dumplings for use in a stew, add 1 tbsp. (15 ml) finely chopped parsley; for dessert dishes, add ½ tsp. (2 ml) finely grated lemon peel and a dash of cinnamon.

at the V.G. than at any other facility in Canada. In 1985, the first liver transplant east of Montreal was performed at the Victoria General Hospital.

The first public school dentist inspection program in Canada was initiated in Halifax in 1907.

Records indicate the first authentic use of chloroform in Halifax took place in 1843.

The Isaak Walton Killam Children's Hospital is also the medical care centre for seriously ill youngsters from the Maritime Provinces.

Sir Sandford Fleming's name is carried on in Fleming Park, a residential area near the "Dingle" on the Northwest Arm of Halifax. Fleming (1827-1915) is credited with the invention of Daylight Savings Time. A man of many talents, Fleming took on the job of chief engineer in the 1880 construction of the Canadian Pacific Railway. He also was instrumental in developing the British Pacific Cable System, making history in the world of communications.

THE FIRST ANNUAL MEETING OF THE CANADIAN BAR Association took place in Halifax in 1897.

The Cunard Shipping Line, which was established in Halifax in 1837, was internationally known as the operator of such magnificent vessels as the Queen Mary and the Queen Elizabeth.

The first Board of Trade in Canada was organized in Halifax in 1750.

With its ideal docking facilities for submarines and warships, Halifax is the home base of two-thirds of the naval branch of the Canadian Armed Forces personnel on the Atlantic coast.

A six-hundred-foot long and nine-foot wide bright blue ribbon wrapped around the Purdy's Wharf office tower in 1985 set a world record. It was cut by Mila Mulroney to officially mark the completion of this impressive downtown Halifax development project.

The first savings bank in Canada, the Collins Bank, started operation in Halifax in 1825.

The first cargo of oil to enter a Canadian port by water arrived in Halifax Harbour on the steamer "Maverick" in 1899.

In May 1986, Halifax hosted the semi-annual NATO conference. This was only the second time that the conference was held in other than the capital city of a NATO member country. Only once before has Canada hosted the NATO conference and that was in Ottawa. The Halifax NATO conference was the biggest security operation ever undertaken by the Province of Nova Scotia, exceeding the extent of security precautions taken when royalty visits.

Hall's Harbour

HALL'S HARBOUR TAKES ITS NAME FROM THE INFAMOUS Samuel Hall, captain of the notorious "Mary Jane" and leader of a privateering band from the American colonies. He used the harbour as a home base for his raids on surrounding settlements.

Vice Admiral Ransford Dodsworth was born in Hall's Harbour in 1866. For his dedication and expertise in building the Turkish navy, he was endowed with a singular honour by that country — he was made a Pasha.

Chipman's Corner, a small Kings County community, was the birthplace of a man who made history in the scientific field. Abraham Gesner was born here in 1797. He developed a process for extracting kerosene from coal, becoming the founding father of the petrochemical industry. The patent for extracting clear-burning oil from the low temperature distillation of coal is registered in Abraham Gesner's name.

Gesner holds a place in Canadian history as the author of the first book on geology in Nova Scotia and New Brunswick and as the founder of Canada's first public museum.

Alfred Fuller was born in the Kings County community of **Welsford** in 1885. The name Fuller became a household word in rural areas all over the country after he organized and operated the Fuller Brush Company.

Welsford was originally known as "The Back Street" until 1864, when John Carmichael renamed it after Major Augustus Welsford, who was killed in the Crimea in 1855 during the storming of the Redan at Sebastopol.

Pasha Rice
(serves 4)

If your pasha has a passion for rice, this dish is sure to please. With its deep, luscious, saffron yellow colour, it is guaranteed to brighten up a meal and tantalize taste buds.

2 cups cooked rice 500 ml
4 tbsp. butter or margarine 60 ml
2 tbsp. slivered almonds 25 ml
4 tbsp. shallots or green onions, chopped 60 ml
1 tsp. turmeric 5 ml

4 tbsp raisins, chopped 60 ml or
4 tbsp. apricots, chopped 60 ml or
4 tbsp. peaches, chopped 60 ml
pinch black pepper

Sauté the shallots or green onions in butter. Add the almonds and turmeric, cooking over low heat for 5 minutes, stirring frequently.

Stir in the rice until the grains are coated with the seasoned butter. Add the fruit and pepper and heat through.

F

LaHave

WITH A SPECIAL BEAUTY AND SERENITY ALL ITS OWN, THE LaHave River winds its way through the scenic countryside of Lunenburg County. Many have called it the "Rhine of Nova Scotia," appropriately so, as many early settlers can trace their roots to Germany.

Four miles east of the mouth of the LaHave River lies the picturesque village of **Kingsburg**. The story goes that so many young Lunenburgers got financial assistance from the thrifty settlers at Kingsburg that it was known in years past as the "Lunenburg Bank."

"The Ovens," situated on beautiful Rose Bay, once yielded gold to the prospector. In fact, it is said that $120,000 worth of gold was gathered here without the use of any sort of drilling machinery whatsoever. The gold is gone now but a natural treasure has been left behind. The jagged cliffs are marked by unique rock formations and deep, oven-like indentations, formed through thousands of years of erosion by the ceaseless, pounding tides. The sea pours into these tunnels and spurts up out of crevices, sending the spray high in the air. This natural phenomenon is well worth a visit. It is thought the first school in Canada was operated in LaHave by the Capuchin fathers in the 1630s.

LaHave Appled Cabbage
(serves 4)

LaHave Appled Cabbage is a somewhat unorthodox treatment for a rather glamourless vegetable. You will enjoy the combination of apples and cabbage and find it delicious served with game, beef or pork.

¼ cup butter or margarine *60 ml*
½ medium sized cabbage, shredded
2 apples, peeled and sliced
salt, to taste
1 tbsp. caraway seed (optional) *15 ml*

Melt the butter in a saucepan and sauté the cabbage for 5 minutes, stirring frequently. DO NOT ALLOW TO BURN! Add the apples and cook for 2 minutes longer. Add the salt, cover and cook for 20 minutes.
Serve garnished with caraway seed.

Note: Unless you are a caraway lover, do not use this rather intense flavouring. However, if you like caraway, it is a wonderfully savoury addition to this dish.

Lunenburg

YOU CAN ALMOST TASTE THE SALT IN THE AIR WHEN YOU visit the port town of Lunenburg. Perched on the shores at the head of Lunenburg Bay, this colourful seaside community has a special flavour all its own.

Lunenburg was the home of the crippled painter Evern Earle Bailley (1903-1977), whose innovative skill was so finely tuned that he learned to paint by holding the brush in his teeth.

Robert Winters, who served as a federal Cabinet Minister in the Liberal Government, was born in Lunenburg in 1910.

The Indians called Lunenburg "the Place of Clams" and when the settlers started to arrive, it became known as "Milky Bay."

Rita Lohnes of the Bluenose Golf Club in Lunenburg won seventeen Nova Scotian or Maritime golf titles in her career.

Between 1940 and 1943, Lunenburg was the location of a Norwegian navy training outfit at Camp Norway. Over 1,500 Norwegian sailors were trained here. The first visit of royalty to Lunenburg came when Camp Norway was inspected by Norwegian King Olav and Princess Marthe.

The Camp Norway site is now used by ABCO, a successful manufacturing company owned by local entrepreneurs, the Eisenhauer family. ABCO has diversified its capacities, manufacturing in its Lunenburg and Mahone Bay factories everything from plastic pipe to vegetable blanchers.

Lunenburg is famous as the home port of the Bluenose, the famous schooner which has appeared on the Canadian dime since 1937. Launched in 1921, the Smith and Rhuland built vessel reigned as Queen of the Sea for eighteen years. After winning four national schooner races, the Bluenose came to a sad end when, laden with a cargo of bananas, she sunk off the Island of Haiti. A replica of the original Bluenose, launched in 1963, is used as a public relations vessel for the Province of Nova Scotia. Bluenose designer William Roue and her Captain Angus Walters, along with the Bluenose itself, have been elected to the Canadian Sports Hall of Fame.

The first recorded use of vaccine in Nova Scotia took place in Lunenburg in 1775. The first child to be vaccinated was a boy named Franklin Bulkley Gould de la Roche.

The replica of the "HMS Bounty" which was featured in the MGM film "Mutiny on the Bounty" was built in Lunenburg.

Jean Baptiste Moreau, the first Anglican missionary to Lunenburg, had a son named Cornwallis. Cornwallis was the first male white child to be born in Halifax.

Reverend Paulus Bryzelius died on Good Friday 1773 while preaching an Easter service at St. John's Church in Lunenburg. He was buried beneath the church's pulpit.

Lunenburg Baked Rice
(4-6 servings)

With each grain nicely browned, this buttery rice dish is a versatile one that seems to taste better each time it is served.

1 cup raw long grain rice *250 ml*
2¼ cups beef broth *575 ml*
½ cup butter or margarine *125 ml*
1 cup sliced fresh mushrooms *250 ml*
1 large onion, chopped
2 tbsp. red or green pepper, chopped *30 ml*

Heat the beef broth and the butter together until the butter melts. Pour into a large casserole dish and add the rice, mushrooms, onion and pepper. Bake, covered, for 30 minutes at 350° F. Remove the cover and continue baking until light and fluffy for about another 30 minutes.

Hint: Save energy by baking this casserole when you are already using the oven for the main course.

F

Nappan

THE FIRST CREAMERY IN NOVA SCOTIA WAS STARTED IN Nappan in 1893.

Nova Scotia has considerable salt reserves which are being mined in both Nappan and Pugwash. Two systems are employed to obtain this useful mineral which has an abundance of uses in addition to enhancing the flavour of our foods. The Nappan mine uses a method which allows water to be pumped into the mine where it dissolves the salt and is then pumped back out and the water allowed to evaporate, leaving behind a high quality salt residue. This operation mines about 300-350 tons a day. The Pugwash plant employs a traditional tunnel mining operation where loads of the unrefined mineral are removed from the mine in large amounts — up to 3,000 tons a day.

As well as being famous for its fossil fields and cliffs, *Joggins* earned a special spot in history when the "Great Log Raft" sailed from Joggins for New York in 1887.

The first experimental farm to be established in Maritime Canada was the Nappan Experimental Farm which commenced operation in 1887. The Farm continues to contribute in the areas of farm management and improved farming methods today as it did one hundred years ago.

Nappan Blueberry Muffins
(makes one dozen medium sized muffins)

These muffins have a fairly cakelike texture and melt in your mouth. The recipe was given to me by Mrs. Roger Bacon, whose husband has been Nova Scotia's agricultural minister for many years. Mrs. Bacon says her husband loves blueberries!

½ cup shortening *125 ml*
1 cup white sugar *250 ml*
2 egg yolks, beaten
2 egg whites, beaten
   until stiff
1½ cups flour *375 ml*

1 tsp. baking powder *5 ml*
½ tsp. salt *2 ml*
1 tsp. vanilla *5 ml*
⅓ cup milk *75 ml*
1½ cups blueberries, fresh or
   frozen, lightly floured *375 ml*

Cream the sugar and shortening together until fluffy. Stir in the egg yolks.
Sift the flour, baking powder and salt together three times.
Add the dry ingredient mixture to the shortening mixture alternately with the milk. Stir until just combined.
Fold in the egg whites and vanilla. Gently stir in the blueberries.
Spoon into a greased muffin tray or use paper cupcake liners. If you wish, you may sprinkle the tops lightly with a bit of sugar.
Bake in a 350° F. oven for 20 - 25 minutes.

Note: Sifting the three dry ingredients refines the flour and allows it to combine quickly with the other ingredients; adding the egg whites separately contributes to the lightness of the batter.

F

Peggy's Cove

PEGGY'S COVE IS, WITHOUT A DOUBT, THE MOST POPULAR spot for tourists to visit in Nova Scotia. Twenty-seven miles from the capital city of Halifax at the mouth of St. Margaret's Bay, it is perched atop weather-beaten, barren, purely rock terrain. This tiny village has the charm and awe-inspiring beauty that draws visitors back time after time.

A unique feature of Peggy's Cove is the fact that it is the only place in Canada to have its post office located in a lighthouse.

Well-known seascape artist William de Garthe made his home in Peggy's Cove. Just before his death in 1983 he completed a magnificent sculpture, carved in the rockface near the roadside, depicting the life of the Village. The 100-foot long sculpture is de Garthe's most lasting tribute to the men of the sea, for whom he had great admiration. It features the figures of thirty-two local fishermen with their wives and children, under the benevolent gaze of a guardian angel.

The Halifax County community of **Hackett's Cove** is the burial place of Janet McDonald, wife of Sergeant Alexander McDonald. The legend surrounding this lady has it that her remains were wrapped in a sheet, or shawl, that once belonged to Bonnie Prince Charlie.

The **Glen Margaret** William Black Memorial Church was built in 1821 entirely by volunteer labour. The church name commemorates Amherstonian William Black, a pioneer Methodist who spread his message throughout Nova Scotia, New Brunswick, Prince Edward Island, and the United States. "Bishop Black," an itinerant preacher, walked from one community to another, with little regard for distance. In fact, it is recorded that he once walked 130 miles from Shelburne to preach in Windsor. The "Father of Methodism" in Nova Scotia died of Asiatic cholera in 1834, when this epidemic swept through Halifax, killing 103 people in three weeks.

Glen Margaret Oatmeal Brown Bread
(makes 2 large loaves or a combination of smaller loaves and rolls)

This recipe was given to me by a friend who lives in the picturesque village of Glen Margaret where she bakes one of the best breads you've ever tasted.

3 cups boiling water *750 ml*
2 tbsp. shortening *30 ml*
1 cup rolled oats *250 ml*
½ cup molasses *125 ml*
1 tbsp. salt *15 ml*
2 tbsp. brown sugar *30 ml*

Combine the shortening, oatmeal, molasses, salt and sugar in a very large bowl. Pour the boiling water over it and allow to cool.

1½ tbsp. yeast *25 ml*
½ tsp. sugar *3 ml*
½ cup warm water *125 ml*

Dissolve the sugar in warm water and add the yeast. Let sit for 10 minutes.

7 - 10 cups white flour *1.75 L - 2.5 L*

Add 2 cups (500 ml) of flour to the oatmeal mixture. Mix well. Add the yeast mixture. Stir vigorously, adding more flour as it is absorbed into the dough.

When the dough becomes too stiff to stir, turn it out onto a well-floured surface and knead until elastic.

Place in a large, greased bowl and grease the top of the dough lightly with shortening. Cover with a clean tea towel and let rise in a warm place until it doubles in size, (about 1½ hours). Punch down the dough with a saucer edge.

Grease the baking pans. Divide the dough into rolls or loaves. Cover and let rise until double. Then pop in the oven and bake at 350° F. for ¾ to 1 hour. The bread is cooked when it sounds hollow when rapped.

Remove the bread from the pans immediately and let cool on a rack. The most difficult part of making bread is disciplining yourself not to cut into it when it is still steaming hot!

F

Port Royal

ANNAPOLIS COUNTY BOASTS THE OLDEST PERMANENT European settlement north of the Gulf of Mexico — the fort at Port Royal dates back to 1605. The building of the fort itself was a tremendous effort at that time and was built "without a nail."

Almost every aspect of society, be it military, religious, scientific, cultural or culinary, is represented by a "first" recorded at Port Royal.

The first social club in North America — the Order of Good Cheer — was organized in 1605, to help pass cold winter evenings in the fort and boost morale when spirits might be flagging. Elaborate dinners were arranged by officers trying to outdo each other. There was a wide variety of seafood, game, and cultivated crops to choose from. Sorrel, chives, shallots, turnips and beets were a few of the species raised in local gardens. Oddly enough, the potato was not planted because it was thought to be poisonous and even to be a cause of leprosy.

The following list of "firsts" shows how historically significant this town is.

- First militia in Canada — 1627
- First graded highway — 1606
- First Roman Catholic Church — 1605
- First surgeon — 1605
- First hospital or sick bay — 1610
- First library in Canada — 1606
- First theatre — "Theatre of Neptune" — 1606
- First play performed — 1606
- First bible class in Canada — 1606
- First baptism — Micmac Chief Membertou — 1611
- First cutlery designed in Canada — 1607
- First recorded daily liquor allowance to workmen in Canada (three quarts of wine per man per day) — 1606
- First stocking of pools with game fish — 1605

After New York was linked with Saint John, New Brunswick, by telegraph, a pony express to **Victoria Beach** provided the vital connection from Britain to the United Sates. Cunard ships brought British dispatches to Halifax. They then were brought 144 miles west by pony express, with fresh horses every twelve miles. Upon arrival at Victoria Beach, they were steamed across the Bay of Fundy to Saint John for relay to New York. This unique communications link was in operation for a short time only in the 1800s.

Good Cheer Vegetable Medley
(serves 6)

The brilliant green colours of the broccoli, leeks and peas are nicely set off by the pale orange sauce and mushrooms. The cheese sauce whips up quickly in a microwave which is also great for cooking vegetables (in a very small amount of water) with no loss of nutrients or texture and an enhancement of natural colour.

1 cup broccoli flowerets *250 ml*
1 cup peas *250 ml*
1 cup leeks, cut in 1-inch (2.5 cm) lengths *250 ml*
1 cup mushrooms, sliced *250 ml*
2 tbsp. butter *30 ml*
2 tbsp. flour *30 ml*
1¼ cups milk *300 ml*
1 cup grated Cheddar cheese *250 ml*

Steam the broccoli, peas, leeks and mushrooms until barely fork tender. Reserve the water in the pan.

Melt butter in a saucepan. Stir in the flour and allow to cook for 3 minutes. Whisk in the milk and, stirring frequently, cook over medium heat until thickened. Beat in the grated cheese.

Place the steamed vegetables in a stovetop casserole dish and pour in the cheese sauce. Add a bit of reserved steaming water until the sauce has a thinnish consistency. Heat through and serve immediately.

M

St. Ann's

THE ST. ANN'S AREA WAS THE SITE OF THE FIRST PERMANENT European settlement in Cape Breton in 1629. The name of St. Ann's probably has some connection with the fact that St. Ann was the patron saint of the Micmac Indians.

The only Gaelic college in North America is located at St. Ann's and was founded in 1939.

Who cares about the one that got away when someone like Commander Hodgson of Montreal can catch whoppers like the one he reeled in from St. Ann's Bay in 1950. The monster bluefin tuna, believed to be the biggest fish caught in the world with a rod and line, weighed 977 pounds.

Isobel MacAulay of St. Ann's was not only instrumental in establishing and promoting the Nova Scotia tartan (designed by Bessie Murray), but she also made the first Nova Scotia tartan kilt.

The Victoria County community of *Englishtown* at the mouth of St. Ann's Harbour was the site of the first Jesuit mission to Cape Breton Island.

Angus MacAskill, the Nova Scotia giant, died at St. Ann's in 1863 at the age of 38 years. Possessing almost superhuman strength, MacAskill was presented to Queen Victoria who declared him "the handsomest man she'd ever seen." MacAskill stood seven feet nine inches tall and weighed 397 pounds.

St. Ann's Spicy Baked Fruit
(serves 6 - 8)

This spicy baked fruit is beautifully presented by serving it in a flan dish but it tastes just as good layered in a casserole dish. It is especially good served straight from the oven with hot or cold ham or poultry.

- **14 oz. can peach halves** *398 ml*
- **14 oz. can apricot halves** *398 ml*
- **14 oz. can pineapple spears** *398 ml*
- **14 oz. can pear halves** *398 ml*
- **1 lemon, sliced**
- **1 cup brown sugar** *250 ml*
- **½ cup vinegar** *125 ml*
- **1 stick cinnamon**
- **1 tsp. lemon rind, grated** *5 ml*
- **1 tsp. salt** *5 ml*

Drain the canned fruit, reserving the juice, which should equal about 3 cups (750 ml).

Bring the juice to a boil, adding the remaining ingredients. Boil for 20 minutes and strain. Pour the juice over the fruit and marinate for several hours or overnight.

Using a large flan pan, arrange the fruit attractively with the pineapple spears serving as the "crust" around the edge, the apricots in a circle inside and with the peaches and pears sharing the centre area. Break the cinnamon stick in half and place it in a cross in the middle of the fruit. Dot with butter and bake uncovered in a 350° F. oven for 30 minutes.

Truro

LOCATED ON THE SALMON RIVER, EAST OF THE HEAD OF Cobequid Bay, the busy industrial town of Truro, has been called the "Hub" of Nova Scotia.

Truro has some historical firsts to its credit. For instance, the first felt hats made in Canada (1866), the first knitted rib underwear in the world (1877), the first long distance telephone circuit in Nova Scotia (1888), and the first circulating library in Canada.

The famous Indian long distance runner, Noel Paul, hails from the Truro area.

Sold under the Reindeer brand, condensed milk went on the market in 1883, manufactured at the first condensed milk factory in Canada, the Truro Milk and Canning Factory.

The process by which films are developed automatically is due to pioneer efforts by Truro native A.W. McCurdy (1856-1923) whose discoveries were put to good use by Kodak.

Called the "Marian Anderson" of Canada, Truro-born (1910) singer Portia White's beautifully trained and controlled voice has thrilled classical music lovers everywhere. She was one of the few women to be photographed by the widely acclaimed photographer, Karsh.

Close to Truro is a Moslem cemetery, said to be the only Mohammedan burial ground in Canada east of Alberta.

Truro is the home of the Nova Scotia Teachers' College which, when it was founded in 1855, was called the Provincial Normal College.

The Honourable Robert Stanfield has his roots in Truro. His distinguished career included serving as Premier of Nova Scotia and as leader of the Progressive Conservative Party of Canada.

Nearby *Bible Hill* is said to have taken its name from the pious nature of an early family of settlers, the Archibalds.

The Nova Scotia Agricultural College is located in Bible Hill. Although it was not established formally by the provincial Legislature until 1899, an experimental farm was established in Truro in 1885.

Truro Green Bean Bake
(serves 10 - 12)

This is a delightful recipe for dressing up green beans. The crunchy almonds and water chestnuts add pizazz to the cheese-sauced vegetables. This casserole is a particularly good addition to a buffet table.

2 12-oz. pkg. green beans, frozen French-cut *2 230-gram pkg.*
1 lb. mushrooms, sliced *500 g*
½ cup butter or margarine *125 ml*
1 onion, small, chopped
¼ cup flour *50 ml*
2 cups milk *500 ml*
1 cup light cream *250 ml*
1½ cups cheddar cheese, grated *375 ml*
1 5-oz. can water chestnuts *1 140-gram can*
⅛ tsp. tabasco *.5 ml*
2 tsp. soy sauce *10 ml*
¼ tsp. salt *1 ml*
½ tsp. pepper *2 ml*
½ cup almonds, slivered, toasted *125 ml*

Thaw frozen beans and drain well.

Melt the butter in a large saucepan and sauté the mushrooms and onions until soft. With a slotted spoon, remove the onions and mushrooms from the saucepan, draining off as much butter as possible. Sift the flour into the butter and, stirring well, cook for a few minutes over medium heat. Whisk in the milk and cream, stirring until thickened. Add the grated cheese and stir until well combined.

Drain and slice the water chestnuts. Add the tabasco, soy sauce, salt and pepper.

Combine the cheese sauce, onions and mushrooms with the green beans in a large bowl. Butter a large casserole dish and pour the mixture into it. Top with the slivered almonds and bake at 350° F. for 35 minutes.

F (unbaked)

Weymouth

THIS DIGBY COUNTY VILLAGE AT THE MOUTH OF THE Sissiboo River was earlier called "Six-hiboux," French for "six owls," a name attributed to the plentiful supply of owls that were in the area.

The famous heavyweight boxer Sam Langford (1886-1956) was born in Weymouth. He drew admiration wherever he fought for his courage, agility and resourcefulness in the ring. Elected to both the Boxing Hall of Fame and the Canadian Sports Hall of Fame, Sam Langford is rated by boxing enthusiasts as the seventh best heavyweight in the history of boxing.

A few miles south of Weymouth lies **Church Point**, appropriately named since the Roman Catholic Church, St. Mary's, is reputed to be the tallest and largest wooden church in North America. It seats 1,800 people and its spire reaches 185 feet in the air and is visible for miles in all directions.

Church Point is located along what has been referred to as the longest main street in the world. The closely populated, largely Francophone section extends along St. Mary's Bay from St. Bernard to Yarmouth.

Church Point is the home of the only French university in Nova Scotia. Founded in 1891, the Université Ste. Anne is fully recognized as a degree-granting institution.

The Ruby, a magnificent sailing vessel built in Church Point and launched in 1878, was last captained by Evelyn E. Robbins. A Yarmouth native, Captain Robbins holds an honoured place in Nova Scotia's trivia file. He was the oldest volunteer to be accepted for service in World War I. The seventy-one year old boasted he could zip through a three hour squad drill followed by an eight-mile march and "jump a fence after it."

The Clare District is one of Canada's major mink producing areas. In fact, the first jet-black mink in the world were bred in this area.

Weymouth Savory Loaf
(makes 2 small loaves)

This unusual savory bread is a surefire combination with chili or spaghetti. The nuts add a bit of texture while the cheese and onion flavours permeate the loaf, giving off a delicious aroma. The bread looks great when it emerges from the oven wearing its three crispy onion rings.

> **2 cups flour** 500 ml
> **1 tsp. salt** 5 ml
> **pinch cayenne pepper**
> **1 tsp. baking soda** 5 ml
> **1 tsp. cream of tartar** 5 ml
> **¼ cup butter** 60 ml
>
> **1 medium sized onion**
> **1 cup grated Cheddar cheese** 250 ml
> **¼ cup walnuts, chopped** 60 ml
> **1 egg**
> **1¼ cups milk** 300 ml

Sift together the flour, salt, pepper, soda and cream of tartar.

Cut in the butter with a pastry cutter.

Peel and slice the onion. Reserve two slices and chop the rest finely.

Add the cheese, onion and walnuts to the flour mixture.

Combine the milk and egg and pour all of the mixture into the dry ingredients. Stir until combined and pour into greased loaf pans.

Top each loaf with three onion rings and bake at 350° F. for about 40 minutes.

Note: One loaf is just enough for a small group of people; the other can be frozen or given to a neighbour or friend.

F

Windsor

IN 1982, HOWARD DILL GREW THE WORLD'S LARGEST PUMPKIN on his farm in Windsor. His champion pumpkin weighed 493½ pounds, and his pumpkin seeds are very much in demand by gardeners all over the country.

Windsor has the distinction of several "firsts":
- First agricultural fair in North America in 1765.
- First English university in Canada — King's College.
- First Masonic home in Canada.
- First four-masted schooner to be built in the Maritimes. The "Uruguay" tipped the scales at 736 tons.
- First steamer to sail up the Avon River commenced her regular trips between Windsor and Saint John in 1832. She was called the "Maid of the Mist."

Gerald Regan, Premier of Nova Scotia between 1970 and 1978, was born in Windsor in 1929.

"Clifton," the home of Judge Thomas Chandler Haliburton, is located in Windsor. A creative satirist and humourist, he invented the character of Sam Slick and the stories of his adventures.

Poet Alden Nowlan, who is known for his realistic and sympathetic treatment of rural Maritime life, hails from Windsor.

The oldest split log blockhouse in Canada was built in Windsor in 1750 as part of the Fort Edward defenses.

Premier of British Columbia and instrumental in the entry of that province into Confederation, the Honourable Amor De Cosmos, who was born in Windsor, changed his unassuming surname of Smith to the more romantic and all-encompassing handle "Amor de Cosmos — lover of the world."

HON. AMOR DeCOSMOS
1858 - 1866

The first student at Windsor's King's College School, the first residential school for boys in Canada, was John Inglis who became the third Anglican bishop of Nova Scotia. Inglis was described as, "next to George IV, the most polished gentleman of his time."

Windsor Pumpkin Muffins
(makes 12 large muffins)

Turn the Hallowe'en jack o'lantern to good use by splitting it in half, scooping out the inner lining (seeds, etc.), inverting it on a large baking sheet and baking at 350° F. until tender. The skin will pull off easily and the pumpkin will be less watery than if boiled.

1½ cups white flour *375 ml*
2½ tsp. baking powder *12 ml*
1 tsp. salt *5 ml*
1 tsp. cinnamon *5 ml*
½ tsp. ground nutmeg *2 ml*
1¼ cups whole bran cereal *300 ml*
⅔ cup milk *175 ml*
¾ cup raisins or blueberries* *200 ml*
1 cup pumpkin, cooked and mashed *250 ml*
½ cup sugar *125 ml*
1 egg
½ cup shortening, softened *125 ml*
1½ tsp. sugar, for topping *7 ml*

* If using blueberries, add them with the dry ingredients.

Preheat oven to 400° F.

Sift the flour, baking powder, salt, cinnamon and nutmeg together in a bowl. Set aside.

Combine the bran, milk, raisins, pumpkin and ½ cup (125 ml) sugar in a large mixing bowl. Let stand until the bran has softened (2 - 3 minutes). Add the egg and shortening and beat well.

Add the dry ingredients all at once and stir until the two mixtures are combined. Do not overmix or the muffins will be tough.

Spoon the batter into a greased muffin pan, filling each cup ⅔ full and sprinkle with 1½ tsp. (7 ml) sugar.

Bake for 35 minutes or until golden brown. Serve warm with lots of butter.

Note: Canned pumpkin may be used in lieu of freshly cooked pumpkin.

Hint: Place paper cupcake liners in the muffin pan instead of greasing the cups.

F

Whycocomagh

BORN IN 1860 IN A TINY COMMUNITY NEAR WHYCOCOMAGH, Jonathan MacKinnon was not only an outstanding Greek Scholar of his time but also editor of the Gaelic newspaper "MacTalla." He is recognized for his translation of many English classics into Gaelic.

The interesting name Whycocomagh is taken from the Indian words meaning "head of the waters or "beside flowing wave tops."

Cape Breton athlete Dr. Hugh MacDonald was born in *Lake Ainslie* in 1856. After achieving success as North American wrestling champion, he returned to Whycocomagh where he practised medicine for forty years.

Born in *Inverness* in 1921, Allan J. MacEachern was appointed Deputy Prime Minister of Canada in 1977, having already served as Minister of Labour, National Health and Welfare, Manpower and Immigration, and as Secretary of State for External Affairs.

Whycocomagh Baked Corn
(serves 6 - 8)

Particularly attractive when green onion and red pepper are used, this tasty dish is an excellent accompaniment to hot or cold ham, chicken or turkey.

- 3 cups corn niblets, cooked 750 ml
- 1 cup grated Cheddar cheese 250 ml
- ¼ cup white or green onion, chopped 60 ml
- ¼ cup red or green pepper, chopped 60 ml
- 1 cup soft bread crumbs 250 ml
- 2 tbsp. melted butter 30 ml
- ½ tsp. salt 2 ml
- ¼ tsp. freshly ground black pepper 1 ml
- ¼ tsp. ground ginger 1 ml
- ¼ cup cream 60 ml

Combine all ingredients in a large bowl and turn out into a buttered casserole dish.

Bake uncovered in a 350° F. oven for 40 minutes.

Note: If you wish, freeze this casserole before baking and thaw before putting in the oven when you are ready to use it.

F (unbaked)

MAIN COURSES

Arcadia

THE YARMOUTH COUNTY COMMUNITY OF ARCADIA IS THE location of a unique building called the "House of Four Peoples", built on the site of an old Micmac camping ground. The house shows features of early French construction and alterations and expansions are by both English and Dutch carpenters. This building is of special interest to our neighbours south of the border as it was here that the famous New England patriot, Paul Revere, was initiated into Freemasonry during a secret visit to Nova Scotia in 1769.

Pinkney Point is of interest to dog lovers as the home of the Nova Scotia Duck Tolling Retriever. This medium-sized golden red dog is the only breed to have been completely developed in Canada.

Surette Island has the distinction of containing the grave of the last survivor of the Acadian deportation from Grand Pré in 1755. This Acadian, who died in 1862, lived to the grand old age of 110 years.

The graveyard of the Church of Immaculate Conception in **East Pubnico** contains the remains of Simon d'Entremont, who in 1839 was the first Acadian elected to the Nova Scotia Legislature.

Pinkney Point Roast Duck
(serves 4)

This is a superb dish and one of the few to eliminate the fat problem that invariably arises when cooking a duck. Although it would be wonderful to be baking a duck retrieved by your very own Nova Scotia Duck Tolling Retriever, a plump "storebought" young duck will do just fine.

4-5 lb. young duck *2 kg*
1 orange, sliced
½ cup orange marmalade *125 ml*
2 tbsp. orange juice *30 ml*

Place a rack in the roasting pan. Prick the duck breast all over with a fork. Cover and place in a 325° F. oven. Drain off the fat periodically so that it doesn't reach above the rack. When the breast juices run clear when pricked with a fork, remove the duck from the oven and place in the refrigerator on a clean platter. Pour the contents of the baking pan into a clean bowl and refrigerate.

About one hour before serving the bird, remove it from the refrigerator, along with the fat, which should be congealed. Scoop off the top fat layer and spoon the precious, gelatinous bottom layer into a clean saucepan. Heat briefly until the jelly liquefies. Stir in the marmalade and orange juice. Set aside.

Remove the giblets from the duck cavity (if you haven't already done so) and place the orange slices inside.

Place the duck in a baking pan and baste it liberally with the marmalade mixture. Put it in a 350° F. oven, uncovered, and bake for about 45 minutes, basting frequently. When the skin has browned, remove the duck from the oven, and carve. Spoon the drippings over individual portions or serve them thickened with a little cornstarch in a gravy boat.

Note: The secret to this recipe is baking the duck twice. The first baking allows the fat to drain through the fork pricks and cooling allows you to separate the delicious drippings from the grease. The second baking yields a beautifully browned skin, sweet with the aroma of oranges.

Dartmouth

THE CITY OF DARTMOUTH IS UNIQUELY BEAUTIFUL WITH ITS twenty-three lakes and numerous public beaches. It represents an amalgamation of nine districts: ***Albro Lake, Burnside, Imperoyal, Lake Micmac, Port Wallace, Tufts Cove, Westphal, Woodlawn,*** and ***Woodside***. Canoeists have put the lakes to good use and representatives from the four Dartmouth canoe clubs — the Banook, Micmac, Senobe and Abernaki — have won numerous times in national and international competitions.

Most people will agree that the name Dartmouth is a distinct improvement on the Indian name for this area — "Boonamoogwaddy," which means "tomcod ground."

The Volvo automobile plant opened in Dartmouth in 1963, with the first Volvo to be manufactured in Canada rolling off the assembly line on June 11 of the same year.

The first iron bridge in Nova Scotia was built in Dartmouth in 1877 with iron parts produced by the Starr Manufacturing Company Limited.

Starr Manufacturing Company Limited also produced another "first" product line. The first spring skates patented in the world were designed by Dartmouthian John Forbes in 1865 and were considered the best to be had in the world at that time. Of the eleven million pairs of skates manufactured by Starr Manufacturing Company, some were shipped as far away as Siberia before the factory closed its doors in 1930.

Formerly called the Mount Hope Asylum, the Nova Scotia Hospital, now considered a leading psychiatric hospital in Canada, was built due in part to the efforts of American humanitarian crusader, Dorothea Dix, who chose the site of the building in 1856.

Buried in the Geary Street Cemetery in 1845, Mrs. Catherine Thompson has one claim to fame. Her niece, Eugenie, became wife of Napoleon III, Emperor of France.

Born in Dartmouth in 1910, Ruby Keeler grew up to be a dancer and an actress. Admired for her accomplishments, few people today realize that her first husband was none other than the famous entertainer Al Jolson.

Dartmouth was named either for the town Dartmouth in Devon, England, or in honour of Sir William Legge, Earl of Dartmouth, who was Colonial Secretary at that time.

Banook Stuffed Spareribs
(serves 4)

Try this recipe on a cold winter's night. You will find the aroma coming from the oven absolutely mouthwatering and the apple-flavoured dressing a perfect complement to the sweetly glazed pork ribs.

2 lb. pork spareribs, trimmed of excess fat *1 kg*

Stuffing:

- 1 cup white bread, cubed *250 ml*
- 1 cup cooked mashed potato *250 ml*
- ½ small onion, chopped
- 2 small apples, peeled cored and grated
- ¾ tsp. sage *3 ml*
- ½ tsp. salt *2 ml*
- ⅛ tsp. pepper *.5 ml*
- ¼ cup butter or margarine, melted *60 ml*

Glaze:

- ⅓ cup honey or corn syrup *75 ml*
- 2 tbsp. brown sugar *30 ml*
- ½ tsp. dry mustard *2 ml*

Mix the stuffing ingredients together.

Either spoon the stuffing into a baking dish and place the spareribs, with the curve inverted, to cover the dressing, *or,* using two pieces of spareribs of equal length, form a cradle under the dressing with one and place the other as a cover over the dressing. Tie around with kitchen string to keep in place.

After the stuffing is in place, rub the upper side of the spareribs with salt and pepper. Place in a 325° F. oven and bake for 2 hours. Meanwhile, mix the glaze ingredients together.

Remove the spareribs from the oven and spread the glaze over the top. Put the meat back in the oven at 350° F. and bake for 15 minutes longer.

Serve by slicing in between the ribs and down through the dressing.

Digby

SITUATED AT THE EXTREME END OF THE ANNAPOLIS VALLEY, Digby, with its ready access to the rich fishing grounds of the Bay of Fundy, is the undisputed scallop capital of North America. Its large fleet of scallop draggers harvest the large, tender, delicious scallops that have made its name famous.

One of the Loyalist refugees who settled in Digby in 1783 was John Edison of Newark, New Jersey. He became town assessor in the newly formed community, and was the grandfather of a very famous inventor, none other than Thomas A. Edison.

In 1875, a former sergeant in the Black Pioneers, Thomas Peters, an African black, was granted one acre of land in Digby. Peters became an active leader in the black community and travelled throughout the area, recruiting people to emigrate to Sierra Leone. His success in this venture led to 1,200 local blacks boarding ship in Halifax to make the long voyage, so filled with hardship that only the strongest survived.

The Digby County settlement called **Marshalltown,** halfway between St. Mary's Bay and the Annapolis Basin, has earned a spot on Canada's cultural map as the home of Maude Lewis. This tiny lady, severely crippled with arthritis, devoted her entire life to painting the cheerful, innocent, rural scenes she loved — on everything in sight, even the doors and windows of the tiny 10 foot by 12 foot cottage she shared with her husband Everett. Born in 1903, Maude Lewis died in Marshalltown in 1970, never dreaming that her brightly coloured, primitive paintings of oxen with eyelashes and one-dimensional tulips would make her name famous throughout the art world.

Charles "Pop" Smith, who was born in Digby in 1856, played second base position in the major baseball leagues between 1880 and 1891. "Pop" just wasn't having a good day when he set a major league record for making five errors in one inning!

In the spring of 1986, the Purina Animal Hall of Fame welcomed a new member, Peaches, an English Setter/Lab mix dog, owned by the Willis and Maxine Marshall family of **Barton**. Peaches showed her intelligence and courage by waking up the Marshalls when she discovered a fire had started in their home.

Digby Scallops Crème de la Crème
(serves 4)

This scallop dish deals a double whammy on the cholesterol and calorie fronts but is absolutely the most wonderful way to serve those incomparable Digby Scallops.

1 lb. scallops *500 g*
2 tbsp. butter *30 ml*
2 tbsp. flour *30 ml*
½ cup **Gruyère cheese,** grated *125 ml*

1½ cups **whipping cream** *375 ml*
2 **egg yolks, beaten**
2 tbsp. **sherry** *30 ml*
⅛ tsp. **lemon pepper** *.5 ml*
½ cup **buttered bread crumbs** *125 ml*

Make sure the scallops are about the same size. Poach them in a small amount of milk or water until they begin to turn opaque. *Do not overcook or they will be tough and flavourless.* Set aside.

Melt the butter in a large saucepan and add the flour. Stir and cook over medium heat for 2 - 3 minutes.

Add the whipping cream and grated cheese to the roux. Whisk thoroughly to combine and cook over low heat until thickened. Remove a couple of spoonfuls of the sauce and add it to the beaten egg yolks. Mix well and return all to the cream sauce mixture. Whisk again and add the scallops, sherry and lemon pepper. Heat gently until hot, stirring frequently. Do not boil.

Pour into a heated casserole dish or ramekins, top with buttered bread crumbs and pop under the broiler until lightly browned.

Note: Adding some of the hot sauce mixture to the beaten yolks will prevent them from solidifying into strings when added to the hot mixture.

Hint: A quick way to get buttered crumbs is to butter the bread before tossing it in the blender.

M B

Halifax

HALIFAX, THE CAPITAL CITY OF NOVA SCOTIA, APTLY christened the "Warden of the North" by Rudyard Kipling, was founded in 1749 by Edward Cornwallis and named in honour of George Montagu Dunk, second Earl of Halifax and president of the Board of Trade and Plantations.

Halifax, situated on a deep, protected harbour which remains ice-free all year round, is a beautiful city with lush parks, busy streets and gracious old homes interspersed with highrise office buildings and ultra-modern hotels.

In 1816 the National School was established on Argyle Street near the Parade Square under the auspices of the Church of England. Records show 117 students enrolled in 1818. This school was the first one in Canada to employ the Madras method of teaching, where the master would teach the senior students who would, in turn, teach the younger children.

Anna Leonowens founded the Victoria School of Art in Halifax in 1887. This institution later became known as the Nova Scotia College of Art and Design and was the first of its kind to be established in Canada.

St. Mary's University, the first English Roman Catholic University in North America, was founded in Halifax in 1832.

Devendra P. Varma, an English Professor at Dalhousie University since 1964, is considered an international authority on Gothic horror. He has republished 217 volumes of rare Gothic romances as well as 200 academic works of his own. Varma is much in demand as an expert on the eerie, bizarre and supernatural.

The historic Halifax Citadel, today operating as one of the most interesting museums in Canada, served as a prisoner-of-war camp for German merchant marines captured in the North Atlantic during World War I.

WHEN CHARLES DICKENS VISITED HALIFAX IN 1842, HE described Canada's first legislative building, Province House, which was built in 1807, as "a gem of Georgian architecture."

The first organized Indian carnival took place in 1760 in Halifax.

Dede, the tragic daughter of Victor Hugo, lived in Halifax from 1861 to 1864 where she hopelessly pursued the object of her affections, a Lieutenant Pinsen, stationed at the garrison. Francois Truffant's acclaimed film, "The Story of Adele H.," details Dede's unhappy life.

The first licensed coffee house in Canada opened its doors in Halifax in 1751.

Harold Rudolph Foster, the creator of the Prince Valiant comic strip, was born in Halifax in 1892.

The first printing press in Canada went into operation in Halifax in 1751.

Maria Morris Miller (1813-1875), a local artist, collaborated with the "Dutch Village Philosopher" and land surveyor Titus Smith in producing a collection called "Wild Flowers of Nova Scotia." Miller's water colour drawings of many of the local species are not only attractive but a serious undertaking in cataloguing Nova Scotian flora. The original series is presently owned by the Nova Scotia Museum.

The first newspaper in Nova Scotia was the Nova Scotia Royal Gazette in 1752.

The play, *The King and I*, was based on the book *Anna and the King of Siam*, which was the true story of Anna Leonowens' sojourn in King Mongkut's court in Siam in the middle 1800s. She lived in the Halifax and **Sunnyside** areas from 1867-1878 and from 1885-1888.

The first tree to be decorated and displayed as a "Christmas Tree" in North America was set up in Halifax in 1846. It is thought that this occurred at 6465 Coburg Road, the residence of a family who had brought this holiday tradition with them from Germany.

Zwicker's Gallery on Doyle Street in Halifax is the first and longest continually operating commercial art gallery in Canada. It had its first showing in 1886 and is well respected in artistic circles today.

Veal Valiant with Mushroom Sauce
(serves 4)

This veal entrée fills the kitchen with the most glorious aroma when cooking. The secret to the delightful smell and the mellow taste of the sauce is, of course, the Madeira wine which provides a perfect foil for the tender blandness of the veal and softens the intenseness of garlic, tomato and onion.

4 serving size portions of veal scallopini
2 tbsp. butter or margarine *30 ml*
1 tbsp. oil *15 ml*
¼ cup flour *50 ml*
salt and pepper
2 cups fresh mushrooms, sliced *500 ml*
4 tomatoes, seeded and skinned
2 garlic cloves, mashed
2 green onions, chopped
2 tbsp. fresh basil, chopped *30 ml* **or**
1 - 2 tsp. dried basil *5 - 10 ml*
4 tbsp. fresh parsley, chopped *60 ml*
1 cup Madeira wine *250 ml*

Heat the butter and oil together in a large frypan. Dredge the veal in flour, seasoned with salt and pepper.

Fry the veal until lightly browned on both sides. Remove from the pan and place on a platter in a warm oven.

Sauté the sliced mushrooms in the same pan, adding more butter if necessary, over high heat until lightly browned.

Remove the mushrooms from the pan and place in a bowl in the oven to keep warm.

Chop the tomatoes and, along with the rest of the ingredients, add to the same pan, stirring gently until the sauce has reduced and thickened.

Return the veal and the mushrooms to the pan and allow to simmer gently in the Madeira sauce for about 5 minutes.

Serve immediately with hot boiled rice and steamed, buttered, shredded zucchini.

Super, Natural Meatloaf
(serves 8)

Filled with nutritious ingredients, this recipe elevates meatloaf from the ordinary to the extraordinary.

2 lb. ground meat* *1 kg*
½ cup bran cereal *125 ml*
2 eggs
1 small can tomato paste
¼ cup milk *60 ml*
3 tbsp. wheat germ *45 ml*

2 carrots, shredded
1 medium onion, chopped
1 garlic clove, minced
2 tbsp. fresh parsley, minced *30 ml*
½ green pepper, diced

* *This recipe calls for ground beef, but a mixture of beef, veal and pork is especially tasty.*

Preheat oven to 350° F.

Combine all ingredients in a large mixing bowl and blend together well.

Lightly pack into a 9 inch x 5 inch (21 cm x 12.5 cm) loaf pan and bake for 1½ hours.

Sauce:

3 tbsp. butter or margarine *45 ml*
1 cup mushrooms, sliced *250 ml*
1 tbsp. green onion, chopped *15 ml*
1 tbsp. cornstarch *15 ml*
1 cup liquid* *250 ml*

* *Choose one or a combination of the following: beef stock, red wine, or Madeira.*

Melt the butter in a saucepan and sauté the mushrooms and green onion until barely tender.

Stir the cornstarch into the liquid and pour into the pan with the vegetables. Bring to a boil, stirring constantly. When thickened, remove from heat.

Slice the meatloaf into 1-inch (2.5 cm) slices and arrange in overlapping fashion down the middle of a platter. Pour the sauce in a stream over the length of the meat and garnish the platter with parsley or green onion wands with the tops feathered.

Lakes of Nova Scotia

LIKE MANY OF NOVA SCOTIA'S INLAND LAKES, *LAKE PONHOOK* has maintained its natural, unspoiled beauty while providing a valuable recreational area for city dwellers. The unusual name comes from the Indian word "bahnook" which means the "first lake in a chain of lakes."

Queens County's *Lake Rossignol* is the largest freshwater lake in Nova Scotia, stretching over twenty miles in length.

In 1984 the Nova Scotia Museum created quite a stir with a prize exhibit, a blue frog. The unusual little fellow was found in *Pine Lake*, Lunenburg County. Although biologists claim blue frogs are not all that rare, this one was a novelty to Nova Scotians.

The *Bras d'Or Lake* in Cape Breton is not really a lake at all. It can best be described as a small, inland sea of 450 square miles. Virtually fog-free, it is extremely popular for boating.

Lake Wallace is about one-third the distance between East Spit and West Spit on Sable Island.

Lake Ponhook Beef Casserole
(serves 4 - 6)

This casserole is a great hit with cheese lovers and makes a satisfying meal when served with a tossed green salad and crusty rolls.

- **1 lb. ground beef, lean** 450 g
- **2 large cans tomato sauce**
- **1 tsp. salt** 5 ml
- **8 oz. egg noodles** 225 g
- **1 cup cottage cheese** 250 ml
- **8 oz. cream cheese** 225 g
- **¼ cup sour cream** 50 ml
- **⅓ cup green onions, chopped** 75 ml
- **1 tbsp. green pepper, minced** 15 ml

Brown the ground beef in a saucepan and add the tomato sauce and salt.
Cook the noodles and drain.
Combine cottage cheese, cream cheese, sour cream, green onions and green pepper.
Layer in a large casserole half of the noodles, all of the cheese mixture, the other half of the noodles, and all of the meat.
Bake at 350° F. for 30 minutes.

Liverpool

Formerly called Rossignol, this pretty Queens County town was renamed Liverpool after Liverpool, England, which, too, is at the mouth of the Mersey River. Liverpool has the oldest town crest in Canada. Depicting a codfish, salmon, pine tree and wheat sheaf, the crest pays homage to the bounteous harvest reaped from the land and sea.

The widely read Canadian historical novelist Thomas Raddall makes his home in Liverpool. Some of his books include *The Governor's Lady, Roger Sudden,* and *The Nymph and the Lamp*.

The Canadian Samuel Pepys, Simeon Perkins, religiously kept a diary between the years of 1766 and 1812. This meticulous record provides a fascinating view of lifestyles, society and events of that time. Some of the original manuscript is displayed at the Perkins House in Liverpool which is operated as a museum.

Clarence Eugene Snow, better known as "Hank" Snow, was born in Liverpool in 1914. His first Canadian success was the song "Blue Velvet" (1937) and his first big United States hit was "I'm Movin' On" which remained on the American hit parade charts for fourteen months.

Liverpool native Enos Collins, whose first job was as a cabin boy, founded the first bank in Nova Scotia and became one of the richest men in Canada. He was also part owner of the famous privateer, the "Liverpool Packet," which captured over one-hundred American ships off the New England coast during the war of 1812.

Launched in Liverpool on April 2, 1905, the steamship "Victorian" was the first large ocean liner to adopt turbine propulsion for greater speed and less vibration. Similar turbines were later used by such vessels as the S.S. Mauretania and the S.S. Queen Mary.

The fish bite with a vengeance in Liverpool! In 1934 Thomas Howell landed a 956-pound tuna, the first tuna of that size ever caught with a rod and reel. Two years later Texan Dr. James Brinkley reeled in a 770-pound man-eating shark, the first one ever caught in this manner in the North Atlantic.

Liverpool Saucy Salmon Loaf
(serves 4)

This salmon loaf holds its shape well and can be refrigerated without losing its flavour. Serve it hot, topped with rich egg sauce, subtly flavoured with dill, or serve it cold, garnished with lemon wedges and fresh dill.

- 1 large can salmon
- 1 can cream of mushroom *or* cream of celery soup
- 1 tbsp. gelatin (one envelope) 15 ml
- 2 eggs
- ¾ cup cracker crumbs (fifteen crackers) 200 ml
- salt and pepper
- 2 tbsp. green pepper *or* celery, finely chopped 30 ml
- 1 tbsp. butter or margarine 15 ml

Drain the salmon and remove the bones.
Beat the eggs and mix in with the other ingredients.
Pour into a casserole dish or loaf pan and dot the top with butter. Bake for 45 minutes at 350° F. or until lightly browned.

Creamy Rich Egg Sauce:

- 1 tbsp. flour 15 ml
- 1 tbsp. butter or margarine 20 ml
- 1 cup milk or cream 250 ml
- 2 eggs, hardboiled and sliced
- salt
- chopped fresh dill
- parsley for garnish

Melt the butter and stir in the flour. Cook gently for 3 or 4 minutes, and then add the milk or cream. Stirring constantly, cook until thickened over medium heat (or microwave).
Stir in salt to taste and a sprinkling of dill. Fold in the egg slices gently. Pour the sauce over the salmon loaf and garnish with parsley sprigs.

Note: This egg sauce is very good with poached, baked or sautéed salmon steaks.

B M (sauce)

Louisbourg

NAMED AFTER KING LOUIS XIV OF FRANCE, LOUISBOURG WAS known as the "Dunkirk of America," drawing a parallel of impregnability between it and the strongly fortified town of Dunkirk in France.

The Louisbourg fort, constructed totally by backbreaking manual labour, was comprised of one-hundred acres of land encircled by twenty-foot thick walls and an eighty-foot wide moat. Thought to be unconquerable by the French who ran it, the huge complex was captured by the British, and in 1760 much of it was demolished by a company of soldiers commanded by Captain John Byron. Interestingly enough, Captain Byron was the father of the British poet and Greek sympathizer who practised a somewhat risqué lifestyle, George Gordon, commonly called Lord Byron.

In the early days, an observatory was constructed at Louisbourg, making it the first one in Canada. Also, the first lighthouse in North America turned on its beacon here in 1734.

In 1725 the pay ship "Le Chameau" went aground approximately fifteen miles off Louisbourg with 310 lives lost. She was discovered in 1965 and yielded one of the richest deep-sea treasures ever to be found. The trove of gold and silver coins was recovered by three Cape Breton divers — Alex Storm, Dave MacEachern and Harvey MacLeod.

Baleine Cove, so named because of a rock formation resembling a whale in the harbour, lies a short distance up the coast from Louisbourg. It was the scene of an interesting historical event on September 5, 1936, when pilot Mrs. Beryl Markham landed her aircraft here. The twenty-five hour non-stop flight from Abington, England, to Baleine Cove, marked the first solo east-to-west Atlantic Ocean flight ever made.

Louisbourg Seafood Casserole
(serves 6)

Filled with its own variety of "treasures" from the sea, this casserole is fit for a king. Light in texture, it refrigerates well.

1½ cups cooked lobster meat, coarsely chopped 375 ml
1 cup cooked crab 250 ml
1 cup cooked shrimp 250 ml
1 cup cooked tuna 250 ml
½ tsp. Worcestershire 2 ml
1 cup celery, chopped 250 ml

2 tbsp. onion, chopped 30 ml
1½ cups mayonnaise 375 ml
½ tsp. salt 2 ml
1 cup breadcrumbs 250 ml
2 tbsp. butter or margarine melted 30 ml

Place the seafood in a large mixing bowl. Add all the remaining ingredients except the crumbs and butter. Toss together lightly.

Spoon into a large casserole dish and top with a mixture of bread crumbs combined with melted butter. Bake at 350° F. for 40 minutes.

Mahone Bay

ALTHOUGH MAHONE BAY WAS KNOWN TO THE INDIANS AS Mush-a-Mush, its name was changed to incorporate the French word "mahonne," which described the low-lying craft used by privateers of the day. In early times, the much feared black flag flying on the mast of a privateer was a frequent sight as the vessels manoeuvred among the 365 tiny islands scattered in Mahone Bay. Mahone Bay is a particularly picturesque spot with its spired churches, numerous fishing boats and old homes clustered around the water.

Rather than surrender to a British ship, a young English deserter blew up the magazine of a privateer vessel, the "Young Teazer," in the waters of Mahone Bay. Twenty-eight members of the crew were killed and the explosion was felt as far as ten miles away. It is said that every June 27, the anniversary of the explosion, a ghostly fireship can be observed flickering in the waters of Mahone Bay.

Nearby **Chester**, whose early settlers came from Massachusetts (1759), is a quiet, charming village and has long been a haven to retired naval admirals, wealthy Americans and city dwellers who make annual pilgrimages to this lovely spot. One such visitor was the Halifax-born diplomat and author Charles Ritchie, who spent many enjoyable summers soaking up the atmosphere at the "Sea Chest," a delightful summer home overlooking the harbour.

Born in Chester in 1904, Dr. Donald Hebb, a distinguished psychologist, is considered to be the father of contemporary neuropsychology. In his lifetime, Professor Hebb received honourary doctorates from fifteen universities and in 1960 was the first Canadian to be president of the American Psychological Association. Always proud of his Maritime roots, Dr. Hebb retired in *Marriott's Cove,* where he died in 1985.

Dude, a seven week-old beagle pup owned by Tim and Janet Oakley of **Chester Basin,** astounded the local vet in December 1985 when he came back to life more than twenty minutes after being declared dead. The "miracle dog" suffered no ill effects from this unique experience.

So called because of the majestic oak trees that once covered it, **Oak Island** was designated Island Number 28 in the first survey done of the Western Shore area in 1785. Documents of the day also show it under the name of Gloucester Island.

Oak Island is a name shrouded in mystery. Legend has it that it was the site where the evil and infamous "Captain Kidd" buried his ill-gotten treasures. The whole idea of buried treasure has captured the imagination of even the most skeptical. For instance, Franklyn D. Roosevelt believed there was truth in this tale and in the early 1900s financed an unsuccessful treasure hunt. Four treasure seekers were killed here in 1965, all in vain, since the soil of Oak Island has not yet yielded her treasure trove.

Mahone Bay Mussels
(serves 2 as an entrée, 4 as a starter)

You may not be muscle bound, but you're bound to enjoy these mussels. This recipe makes an enjoyable meal for two when served with a spinach salad and chunks of crusty French bread.

2 lb. mussels in the shell *1kg*
2 tbsp. butter *30 ml*
1 onion, chopped
2 cloves garlic, minced
1 tbsp. parsley *15 ml*
½ cup white wine *125 ml*
juice of ½ lemon
1 bay leaf
¼ tsp. thyme *1 ml*

Scrub the mussels in the shell, rinsing a few times in cold running water. Discard any damaged or open mussels.

Bring the remaining ingredients to a boil and add the mussels. Cover the pot and cook until mussels start opening. Stir once or twice.

Serve the mussels with melted butter or with the cooking broth (after it has been strained twice through cheese cloth) or plain. (If serving with the broth, you may wish to season it with a little salt and pepper.)

Note: Mussels are amazingly inexpensive.

M

Malagash

THE COMMUNITY OF MALAGASH ON TATAMAGOUCHE BAY got its name from the Indian word "malegawach," which meant "a place where people meet to play games."

The first salt mined in Nova Scotia was hoisted from a Malagash mine in 1918.

Hans Jost, who has brought to Nova Scotia the skills of a long line of European grape growers, operates Jost Wineries in Malagash. Jost says this area along the Northumberland Strait is ideal for grape cultivation because of its long growing season, moderate temperatures and the frost protection afforded it by the Strait's shallow waters. Jost Vineyards Limited had their first wines featured in Nova Scotia liquor stores in 1985.

The quiet Colchester County community of *New Annan* was the birthplace of Anna Swan in 1846. Pretty and well-educated, she travelled extensively with P.T. Barnum's Greatest Show on Earth. Standing 7'11" tall, she married a man of like proportions, Captain Martin van Buren, an American employed with P.T. Barnum. Anna Swan bore two children, both of whom died in infancy. It is thought that one of the babies, who weighed twenty-three and one-half pounds was the largest recorded live birth in history.

JOST VINEYARDS

COMTESSA

WHITE WINE VIN BLANC

750 ml 11% alc./vol.

A semidry, delightful wine, made in the Rhinewine Tradition from Vinifera and Interspecific Grapes.

PRODUCED AND BOTTLED BY
JOST VINEYARDS LIMITED MALAGASH NOVA SCOTIA CANADA

Product of Canada   Produit du Canada

+160200

Tatamagouche Bay Herbed Chicken Breasts
(serves 2)

Poached in wine stock, the delicate flavour of the chicken breasts is enhanced by a fresh herb sauce.

2 large chicken breasts, halved, boned and skinned
¼ cup white wine *60 ml*
¼ cup water *60 ml*
salt and freshly ground pepper

Sauce:

2 egg yolks
⅓ cup whipping cream *75 ml*
2 tbsp. fresh herbs,* *finely* **chopped** *25 ml*
1 tsp. lemon juice *5 ml*

* *Use some or all of the following: tarragon, basil, parsley, thyme, chervil, savory, and/or dill.*

Place the chicken in a small saucepan with a cover. (I find a small Corning Ware casserole dish is just the right size.)

Add the wine and water and season lightly with salt and pepper. Cover and bring to a boil. Reduce the heat and simmer gently for 7 - 10 minutes. Set aside in a warm oven.

In a double boiler (a microwave works well for this job) combine the egg yolks with whipping cream and ⅓ cup of cooking liquid from the chicken. Place over simmering water and stir vigorously with a whisk until the sauce is thick and creamy. Stir in the herbs and lemon juice and some salt and pepper until the sauce tastes just right.

Lift the chicken breasts out of the cooking pan with a slotted spoon and place on a platter. Pour the creamy herb sauce over and serve immediately.

M (Sauce)

Milton

THE FIRST CANADIAN AUTHOR TO SELL MORE THAN ONE million copies of a book was Margaret Marshall Saunders. Born in the Queens County community of Milton, Saunders has twenty-five books to her credit and is best known for *Beautiful Joe,* which she published in 1894. It was a huge success, not only selling a million copies but also being translated into fourteen languages. Saunders was an animal lover who donated most of her royalties to animal protection agencies.

Dr. Francis Magoun, born in Milton in 1899, had a successful career with Standard Oil. A brilliant scientist, Dr. Magoun held forty-four patents for his own inventions.

A homesick sheep, anxious to set hoof on dry ground, jumped overboard as DeMonts was sailing in the coastal waters off what is now known as **Port Mouton**. To commemorate this 1604 event, DeMonts christened the place Port Mouton. This name stuck and the Indian name of Wologumk faded from memory.

Port Mouton Rack of Lamb
(serves 6)

This recipe calls for a rack of lamb cooked to the medium rare stage. If you prefer well-done lamb, lengthen the baking time to 30 minutes per pound. Dusted with herbs and accompanied by a full-bodied sauce, this lamb falls into the gourmet category.

1 rack of lamb
2 garlic cloves, cut in slivers
freshly ground black pepper
rosemary
mint
salt

¼ cup mint sauce (bottled) *60 ml*
½ cup molasses *125 ml*
½ cup Dijon* mustard *125 ml*
½ cup red wine vinegar *125 ml*

* *Prepared mustard is acceptable.*

Make slits in the outer layer of fat and insert the slivers of garlic, pushing them in completely.

Place the rack of lamb, fat side up, in a small roasting pan. Season with a generous sprinkling of pepper, rosemary, mint and salt. Place in a 400° F. oven for 15 minutes. Remove the lamb from the oven and baste with the mint sauce.

Return to the oven, lowering the temperature to 350° F. Bake for 15 minutes.

Mix the molasses, mustard and vinegar together. Remove the lamb from the oven and baste generously with this mixture.

Return the rack of lamb to the oven for an additional 30 minutes, basting occasionally with the pan drippings and additional molasses mixture.

Remove the lamb from the oven and place on a warmed platter.

Heat the juices remaining in the pan, adding red or white wine, water or stock to create more juice.

Serve the lamb with the pan drippings poured over each juicy, succulent slice. Superb!

Pictou

ONE OF THE LARGEST LIVE LOBSTER PRODUCING AREAS IN the world, Pictou, which is located on the northwest side of Pictou Harbour, takes its name from the Micmac word "Piktook," which means "an explosion of gas."

Dr. Thomas McCulloch (1777-1843), a Pictonian educator, was the first president of Dalhousie University, serving from 1838 to 1843, when he died in office. He had a keen interest in biology which is reflected by the impressive McCulloch collection of mounted birds which is presently on display at the Life Science Building of Dalhousie University. This man of many talents was also the author of the first Canadian literary work in humour. He wrote a series called "Letters of Mephibosheth Stepsure" which appeared in the "Acadian Recorder" in the 1820s.

The "Royal William" was the first steamship to cross the Atlantic Ocean, and she did so from Pictou to London, England, in 1833. The "Royal William" also holds the record for being the first British steamship to enter Boston Harbour. Later sold to Spain and renamed the "Isabella Secunda," she was refitted as a warship and became the first steam-powered warship to fire guns.

Pictou was the home of Group Captain Elem Fullerton, who accompanied Roald Amundsen over the North Pole in 1922. One year prior to that he flew the first airplane over the North Pole.

In 1820 Pine Hill Divinity College was opened in Pictou; however, it later moved to Halifax.

In 1983, a German Shepherd dog named Maude rescued three-year-old Debbie Chisholm from the icy waters of Pictou Harbour. Maude is now a member in good standing of the Purina Animal Hall of Fame.

Between 1845 and 1905, 6,000 sheep and cattle died in the Pictou area due to poisoning from ragwort or "Stinking Willie," an evil-smelling weed. The epidemic lasted for a long time because investigators had difficulty finding the cause, and "Stinking Willie" spread like wildfire through fields and pastures.

Many Cape Bretoners of Scottish descent can trace their roots to Pictou, "the Birthplace of New Scotland," where the first boatload of Scottish Highlanders arrived on the "Hector" in 1773.

Pictonian George Mercer Dawson (1849-1901) was involved in much of the initial exploration efforts in British Columbia and the Yukon. The city of Dawson in the Yukon Territory takes its name from this intrepid explorer.

Pictou Pineapple Glazed Ham
(serves 4)

Very simple to prepare, this ham dish is quite delicious. The mustard, pineapple juice and brown sugar mingle together to form a nicely balanced sauce, gently flavoured with the spiciness of whole cloves.

1½ - 2 lb. ham, in a thick slice *1 kg*
2 tsp. prepared mustard *10 ml*
1 cup pineapple juice *250 ml*
½ cup brown sugar *125 ml*
6 whole cloves
6 slices pineapple
6 maraschino cherries

Put the ham in a baking dish. Spread with prepared mustard and pour the pineapple juice over it.
Sprinkle with the brown sugar and stick with the whole cloves.
Bake at 350° F. until tender (about 1 hour).
Remove from the oven and lay the six slices of pineapple over the ham. Drop a cherry into each pineapple hole and return the pan to the oven. Bake until delicately brown at 400° F., basting frequently with the pan juices.

River John

ANNA SUTHERLAND BISSELL, A RIVER JOHN NATIVE, WAS THE driving force behind the development of the Bissell carpet sweeper. Established in 1874, the Bissell Corporation has become a household word throughout North America.

James Chalmers Bigney, born in the River John area in 1892, could, at the age of twenty-two, backlift 3,800 pounds. He could also hold horizontally in his teeth a three-foot-long handle with a twenty-pound sledge hammer on the end of it. He could control four horses, hitched in pairs, pulling in opposite directions. Yet, he was only 5'6" tall and weighed less than 200 pounds. When asked the reason for his outstanding abilities, he simply said: "I was born strong." He later moved his family to Tufts Cove and his son Nathan, "a chip off the old block," was said to be the strongest man in the Royal Canadian Navy in World War II.

In 1880, the Murray family of *Little Egypt* were astonished when Mrs. Murray gave birth to quintuplets. Unfortunately, all died shortly after birth.

Little Egypt Chicken
(serves 6)

With its brilliant yellow peaches, red tomatoes, and green pepper strips nestled in a tangy sauce among lightly browned chunks of chicken, this dish is very appealing to the eye and will tempt the most flagging appetite. Fit for a pharoah!

1 chicken, cut up	2 tomatoes, cut in wedges
½ cup flour 125 ml	1 large green pepper, cut in thin strips
½ tsp. salt 2 ml	1 large onion, chopped
¼ tsp. pepper 1 ml	2 sticks celery, chopped
½ tsp. paprika 2 ml	1 tbsp. soy sauce 15 ml
3 tbsp. oil 45 ml	3 tbsp. vinegar 45 ml
1 large can peaches	1 tbsp. cornstarch 15 ml

Mix the flour, salt, pepper and paprika in a large plastic bag. Add the chicken parts, one at a time and shake until well coated.

Pour the oil to sauté the chicken into a large deep frying pan or a Dutch oven, if you have one. Brown both sides lightly. Pour off any excess oil. Add the green pepper, onion and celery to the pan. Cover and cook over medium heat until the onions are transparent.

Meanwhile, drain the peaches and mix the soy sauce, vinegar and cornstarch into the peach syrup. Pour over the chicken and add the peach slices and tomatoes. Stir gently occasionally as the sauce thickens over low heat.

Serve over hot buttered rice.

Note: This dish can be refrigerated and heated up again the next day, if you are fortunate enough to have any leftovers.

Shelburne

THE FIRST FRENCH SETTLERS NAMED THIS AREA PORT Razior, the English renamed it Port Roseway, and Alexander McNutt, in 1765, was granted 100,000 acres of land and called it New Jerusalem. The name Shelburne was first used in 1783 in honour of the Earl of Shelburne, British prime minister from 1782 to 1783.

In 1783, a great influx of Loyalists caused the population to soar, making Shelburne one of the largest settlements in North America at that time.

To accommodate the youngsters during Shelburne's boom period, schools were organized with records showing a total of twelve different schools operating in 1791.

Nearby *Jordan Falls* was the birthplace of Donald McKay in 1810. McKay is famous for building some of the finest American clipper ships that ever put to sea. To his credit are such famous names as *The Flying Cloud* and *The Sovereign of the Seas*. It has been said his ships were the fastest to sail under any flag. In a busy life devoted to designing the new breed of clipper ship, McKay took time out to father twenty-one children.

Now operated as a museum, the Ross-Thompson House in Shelburne is the only known surviving eighteenth century store in Nova Scotia. Originally owned by the Ross brothers and operated by their manager, Thompson, the store started as a ship's chandler operation and branched into other enterprises to make a profit for its operators.

Marjorie Bailey Brown of **Lockeport** established four Canadian track records during her career.

At the time when enemy warships roamed British waters, the brave and ingenious **Rood's Head** womenfolk learned of the approach of a hostile vessel. The town's menfolk were away and these pioneer women decided they would not give up their little settlement without a fight. They dressed themselves and their older children in red cloaks and lined up on Rood's Head Bluff with "military" broomsticks held high. One lady marched up and down, beating out a rousing rhythm on a drum. Shots were fired seaward from all available weapons and the threatening vessel withdrew immediately.

Nearby **Birchtown** was the first rural black community in North America. Settled by 1,000 blacks in 1783, it took its name from General Birch.

Christ Church in Shelburne has the distinction of being the first church in British North America to be consecrated (1790).

Shelburne Baked Sole
(serves 4 - 6)

This baked sole, prepared with a delicately seasoned sauce, retains its moisture and flavour. If you like lots of sauce, add half as much again of each sauce ingredient.

1½ lb. fillets of sole 750 g
½ lb. mushrooms 225 g
2 tbsp. butter or margarine 30 ml

Sauce:

2 tbsp. butter or margarine 30 ml
1 tbsp. flour 15 ml
½ cup milk 125 ml
3 tbsp. sherry 45 ml
2 tsp. grated onion 10 ml

2 tsp. fresh parsley, chopped 10 ml
½ cup Parmesan cheese, grated 125 ml
dash cayenne or lemon pepper

Melt 2 tbsp. (30 ml) of butter in a fairly large, shallow baking dish. Place the fillets in the dish, turning them to coat in the melted butter. Sprinkle generously with salt and pepper. Bake in a 350° F. oven for 5 minutes.

Meanwhile, slice the cleaned mushrooms and sauté in a small amount of butter over high heat. Remove from the pan with a slotted spoon and place on top of the fillets which have just been removed from the oven.

In the same saucepan used to fry the mushrooms, melt 2 tbsp. (30 ml) of butter and blend in the flour. Add the milk and sherry and cook, stirring constantly, until thickened. Stir in the grated onion, parsley, pepper and Parmesan cheese. Continue cooking for about 2 minutes. Add salt to taste. Spread the sauce over the mushrooms and fish.

Bake at 350° F. for 20 minutes. Before serving, place under the broiler for a couple of minutes to brown lightly. Watch carefully to avoid burning.

M (Sauce)

Springhill

THE CUMBERLAND COUNTY TOWN OF SPRINGHILL WAS SO named because the hill on which the town was built once contained many springs of fresh water.

Springhill is the hometown of Anne Murray, the popular singer who soared to fame with her hit single "Snowbird." Murray was the first Canadian female vocalist to earn a gold record.

Springhill native Johnny Mooring was the first Nova Scotian to win the International Fiddling Championship (1964). He also won the North American Fiddling Championship for three consecutive competitions.

Among the works composed by the Springhill-born (1899) pianist Trevor Morgan Jones is a composition entitled "Symphony to Halifax," which was commissioned for the 1949 Bicentennial celebration.

The first trade union legalized in a Canadian colliery was organized in Springhill in 1879.

Over the years, Springhill has had more than its fair share of heartache and disaster, mainly in connection with the mines. In 1891, 125 miners died in an explosion in Cumberland's Number One shaft. In 1956, 39 men were killed in the Number Four Colliery explosion. Springhill was devastated by a $1.5 million fire in 1957. In 1958, a subterranean earthquake, severe enough to be recorded on the Dalhousie seismograph 100 miles away, shook Cumberland's Number Two shaft. 174 men were trapped in the mine by its force. During a fourteen-day vigil, 100 of the 174 men were rescued. As a matter of interest, in 1958, a Springhill miner brought home $13 per day.

No doubt the name *Mapleton* is directly related to the wonderful maple syrup produced in and around this community. In fact, Cumberland County produces most of the maple syrup harvested in Nova Scotia — about 8,800 gallons each year.

Will R. Bird, the well-known Nova Scotian writer who has twenty-seven books to his credit, and is best known for his travelogues and historical romances, hails from **East Mapleton**.

Springhill Stuffed Pork Chops
(serves 4)

This recipe yields a succulent, tender pork chop, blanketed with creamy gravy and topped with crisped savory dressing.

4 thick pork chops
3 cups soft bread crumbs 750 ml
2 tbsp. onion, finely chopped 30 ml
¼ butter or margarine melted 60 ml
¼ cup water 60 ml
¼ tsp. poultry seasoning 1 ml
1 apple, peeled, cored and grated
1 can cream of mushroom soup
⅓ cup water 75 ml

Trim the chops of excess fat and brown lightly in a bit of oil on both sides. Place in shallow baking dish.

Mix together the bread crumbs, onion, butter, ¼ cup (50 ml) water, apple and poultry seasoning.

Using your hands, shape the dressing into four mounds and place one on top of each pork chop.

Mix the soup with ⅓ cup of water. Spoon over the chops and dressing. Bake at 350° F. for 1 hour.

Hint: Poultry seasoning is a versatile flavouring and one that is underused. It adds a nice touch to casseroles, gravies and stuffings.

B FP

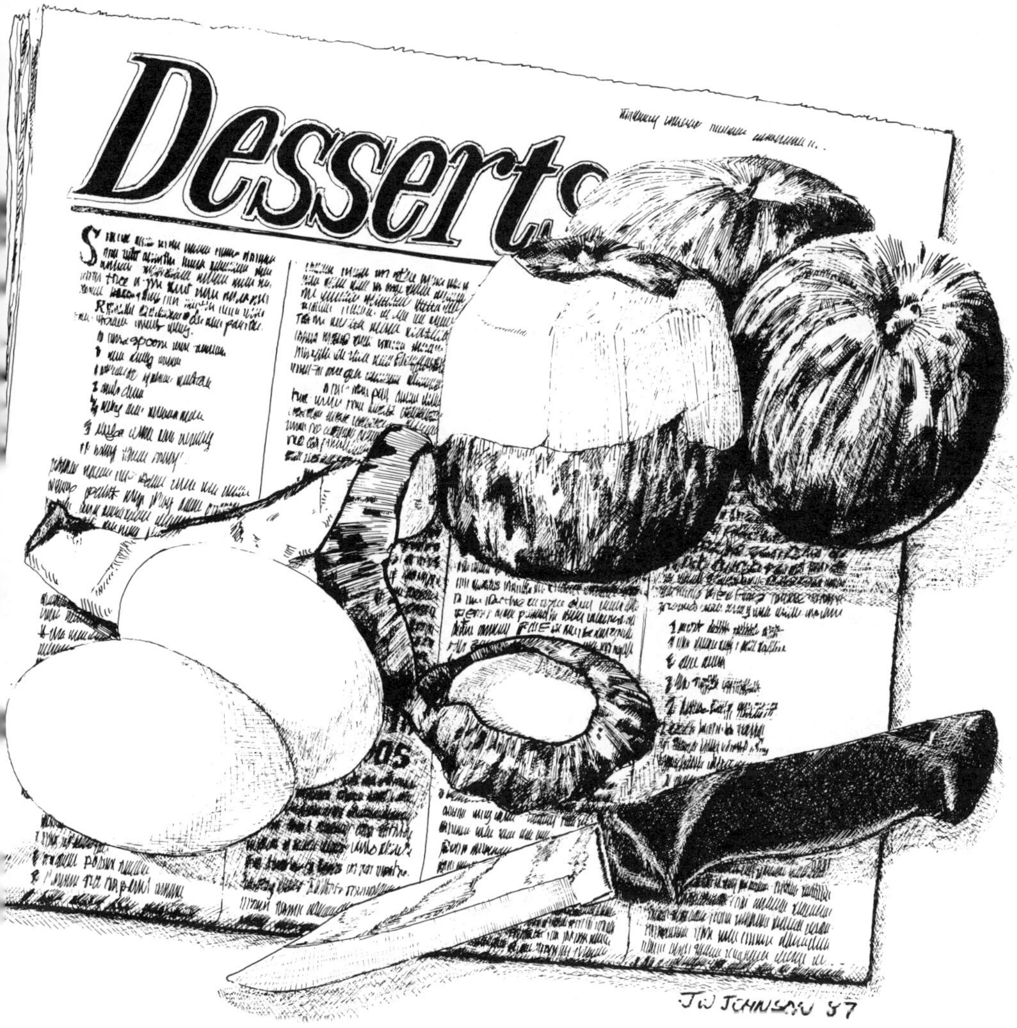
Desserts
JW JOHNSON '87

Advocate

Located on Advocate Harbour near Cape d'Or, this community was the site chosen by settlers originally planning to land at Apple River. Tradition has it that someone in the group said, "I advocate the selection of this harbour." Everyone agreed and the name Advocate has stuck ever since.

A unique rock formation called the "Three Sisters" can be seen in this area. The name comes from the legendary Glooscap tale of three sisters who were turned to stone.

Fred Simpson Cameron, winner of the Boston Marathon in 1910, was born in Advocate in 1886.

Nearby *Spencer's Island* was the building site for the mystery ship — the Mary Celeste. Launched as the Amazon in 1861, she was renamed the Mary Celeste in 1868 and set sail from New York for Genoa, Italy, with Captain Benjamin Briggs in charge. Accompanying Captain Briggs and the crew were his wife and daughter. None of them was ever seen again. A few weeks after the ship's departure from New York, the Mary Celeste was brought into the Port of Gibraltar, having been discovered floating off the Azores, with not a soul on board. Found with plenty of provisions and an intact cargo, there were no signs of fire, struggle or panic aboard. The ill-fated Mary Celeste, after a succession of owners, finally ran aground in Gonave Channel, Haiti, in 1885. The mystery of the Mary Celeste has triggered the imagination of all who hear her story and in 1935, Hollywood produced a film starring Bela Lugosi. It was simply called *The Mystery of the Mary Celeste*.

Spencer's Island Chocolate Mounds
(makes 4 dozen cookies)

These chocolatey mounds are attractive with dustings of white icing sugar and crackly surfaces. Served with a glass of cold milk for a snack, they have a way of disappearing into thin air.

- 1½ cups white sugar 375 ml
- ½ cup mayonnaise 125 ml
- 4 squares *unsweetened* chocolate, melted
- 2 eggs
- 2 tsp. vanilla 10 ml
- 2 cups white flour 500 ml
- 2 tsp. baking powder 10 ml
- ¼ cup icing sugar 50 ml

In a large bowl beat the first five ingredients for 2 minutes with a mixer or until well combined by hand. Stir in the flour and baking powder. When thoroughly mixed, roll the dough into ½ inch (12 mm) balls. Roll each one in the icing sugar.

Place the balls two inches (5 cm) apart on ungreased cookie sheets.

Bake in a 350° F. oven for 12 minutes.

F

Amherst

Dubbed "BUSY AMHERST," THIS STRATEGICALLY LOCATED town lies on the Isthmus of Chignecto between the Nappan and Missaguash Rivers and overlooks the fertile Tantramar marshes (said to be the largest in the world) which comprise eighty square miles of prime farmland in Nova Scotia. Originally called "Les Planches" by French settlers, the town was renamed after Lord Jeffrey Baron Amherst, a well known military commander who became Governor of Virginia.

During the First World War, a prisoner-of-war camp in Amherst had among its number a man who played a key role in the Russian Revolution — Leon Trotsky. When he mentioned his incarceration here for a short time in 1917 in his autobiography, it was in the most distasteful of terms. He said that imprisonment at the Amherst Camp rivalled even a term at the dreaded Fortress of St. Petersburg.

The author Wyndham Lewis was born in his American father's yacht off Amherst in 1882 — a unique way to ensure dual citizenship status!

Two Nova Scotian Premiers were native Amherstonians. The Honourable Edgar Rhodes served his province between 1925 and 1932, while the Honourable William Pipes held office from 1882 to 1884 and again in 1850.

In 1879, *The Haunted House,* which ran to ten editions, was published. Authored by Walter Hubbell, it documented the supernatural goings-on in a home on Princess Street where eighteen-year-old Ester Cox lived with her aunt and uncle. At the time of the bizarre haunting, the Princess Street home became the focal point for psychic investigators, the curious and opportunists like Hubbell who organized a touring show featuring Ester Cox who he claimed would perform poltergeist tricks on stage.

The first plant on the continent to manufacture electricity from coal went into operation in Amherst in 1907.

Four fathers of Confederation have connections with Amherst. Sir Charles Tupper, Prime Minister of Canada for less than three months in 1896, was born here in 1821. Jonathan McCully, Edward Chandler and Robert Dickey lived in Amherst and the Dickey family home, Grove Cottage, 150 Church Street, is now the Cumberland County Museum.

Amherst strong man John "Moose" Kent was an excellent drawing card to one of the Maritime Winter Fairs held in that town. An advertised feature of the Fair was "Moose" Kent's promise to fly to Halifax. When the big day came, "Moose" strapped on wings (probably of iron) and jumped off the roof of a building in full view of a large excited crowd. He did survive the fall and lived out the rest of his life in Amherst, well-known as a local character.

Born just outside Amherst in 1926, Papa Joe Brown, leader of the popular country folk group Family Brown, was recognized for his outstanding contribution to country music in Canada and continued to perform until the day he died in 1986.

Henry George Ketchum nearly saw his dream for the Chignecto Ship Railway come true. Docks were constructed at Fort Lawrence and Tidnish where ships were to be hydraulically lifted onto rail beds and transported seventeen miles across the Isthmus of Chignecto. Work was commenced on this railway in the 1890s, the first of its kind in North America. After four million dollars were spent, a change in government saw his project grind to a halt, never to be completed.

Amherst Old Fashioned Cream Puffs
(makes 1 dozen small cream puffs)

This recipe came from my grandmother Robbins' well worn, food-spattered cookbook. Grandma was born in 1870 and raised a large family, even by old-fashioned standards. You can be sure that a tremendous number of cream puffs were enjoyed by the Robbins family and Grandma's original recipe still tastes as good today as it did then.

½ cup butter *125 ml*
1 cup boiling water *250 ml*
1 cup flour *250 ml*
½ tsp. salt *2 ml*
½ tsp. sugar *2 ml*
4 eggs

Add the butter to the boiling water and when this comes to a hard, rolling boil, add the flour all at once. Stir vigorously until the batter leaves the sides of the pan and forms a ball.

Mix in the salt and sugar and cool. Add the unbeaten eggs one at a time, beating thoroughly after each addition.

Grease the baking sheet and drop balls of dough the size of a walnut, or larger, three inches apart.

Bake in a 350° F. oven for 30 minutes, when puffs should appear risen and lightly browned. Turn the oven off and leave the puffs in the oven until they cool. This allows the puffs to dry out so they will not collapse.

When cool, slit the puffs open with the kitchen shears and spoon in sweetened whipped cream or chocolate cream pudding. Decorate with a drizzle of melted semi-sweet chocolate or a generous sprinkling of icing sugar.

Note: Cream puffs can be made in many shapes and sizes. Small, round ones can be used as casings for chicken or seafood salads. Tiny ones, shot full of whipped cream or vanilla custard can be clustered together and dusted with cocoa or icing sugar for a delightful light dessert. If you plan to fill the puff cases with a savoury rather than a sweet filling, omit the sugar from the puff recipe.

F (unfilled)

Annapolis Royal

ANNAPOLIS ROYAL IS A PEACEFUL TOWN, WITH TREE-LINED streets, well-preserved homes and a Historic Garden Development Project, which attracts many visitors. Annapolis Royal was so named to honour Queen Anne and the ending "polis" is from the Greek word meaning city. Royal was added to incorporate part of Port Royal, the name once used to refer to the land area encompassing the actual town site.

Until it was replaced by Halifax, Annapolis Royal served as the capital of Nova Scotia from 1710 to 1749.

Annapolis Royal is a town of historical firsts. A few of them are:
- First police force (1734)
- First bowling green (1734)
- First common law courts
- First Justice of the Peace
- First English school teacher in Canada licensed by Great Britain (1729) — the Reverend Richard Watts
- First black female mayor in Canada, Daurene Lewis was elected in 1984. Her father, James A. Lewis, was the first black Lions Club member in Canada.

Morris Robinson, the first president of the Mutual Life Insurance Company of New York, was born in Annapolis Royal in 1784.

Annapolis Royal's Garrison Cemetery, considered to be the oldest English cemetery in Canada, has superb examples of early Nova Scotian gravestone art, dating back to 1720.

The small neighbouring community of *Lequille* is the site of the first water-powered grain grinding grist mill in North America. It commenced operation in 1607.

The Annapolis Tidal Power Generating Station, an experimental project harnessing the remarkable Bay of Fundy tides to produce electricity, went into operation in 1984. It is at present the first and only one of its kind in the western hemisphere and one of a very few in the world.

In 1738, Major Erasmus James Phillips founded the first Masonic Lodge in Canada in Annapolis Royal.

Annapolis Royal Apple Squares

The apple is Nova Scotia's most popular dessert fruit. Of the multitude of apple recipes I have tried over the years, this one stands out as being remarkably delicious.

Crust Mixture:

¾ cup butter *200 ml*
1 cup brown sugar *250 ml*
1¾ cups oatmeal *450 ml*
1½ cups flour *375 ml*
¼ tsp. baking soda *1 ml*
dash salt

Filling:

2½ cups apples, thinly sliced* *625 ml*
2 tbsp. butter *30 ml*
½ cup sugar *125 ml*
¾ tsp. cinnamon *3 ml*

* *Five medium-sized apples should be enough. When measuring, be sure to pack the slices down tightly in the measuring cup.*

Lightly grease a 9-inch square (21 cm square) pan.

Cream the butter and sugar together and add the remaining ingredients for the crust. Mix until well combined.

Press two-thirds of the crust mixture into the pan. Place the apples on top. Dot with the butter and sprinkle with the sugar and cinnamon. Cover evenly with the remaining oat mixture.

Bake for 40 - 45 minutes in a 375° F. oven. The crust should be lightly browned and the apples softened.

F

Arichat

LOCATED ON THE NORTH SIDE OF ISLE MADAME IN Richmond County, this community was, for a time, known as Port St. Mary's.

In 1969, an Arichat native won the Canadian and North American college music titles. Her name was Cornelia Boucher and she competed for these titles with over 10,000 finalists from 1,000 different universities.

An ecologist's nightmare came true on February 3, 1970, when the tanker "Arrow" ran aground on **Cerberus Rock** in Chedabucto Bay. One and one-half million gallons of oil spilled into the Strait of Canso.

In 1918 **Grande Anse** grew in importance as a resource area for sphagnum moss. The moss was harvested from local bogs, packed and shipped overseas to be used as effective dressings for wounded soldiers in World War I.

St. Peter's, a village on a narrow strip of land between St. Peter's Inlet and St. Peter's Bay, was the home of Dr. George U. Hill (1918-1969). Honoured with the Distinguished Flying Cross, Dr. Hill was credited with shooting down at least sixteen enemy planes during World War II.

The Lone Shieling, a replica of a Scottish crofter's hut, nestles among 300-year old sugar maple trees in the Grande Anse River Valley.

St. Peter's Chocolate Mousse
(serves 4)

It is truly a marvel that this heavenly dessert can be prepared so quickly! Mousse recipes are often complicated but St. Peter's Chocolate Mousse requires only 30 minutes of chilling before serving.

> **6 oz. semi-sweet chocolate chips** *175 g*
> **⅓ cup coffee, strong and boiling hot** *100 ml*
> **2 eggs**
> **1 tbsp. rum *or* vanilla** *20 ml*
> **1 cup whipping cream** *250 ml*

Optional: additional whipping cream and chocolate curls for garnish.

In a processor fitted with a steel blade, blend the chocolate and coffee until the chocolate is melted. Add the eggs and rum and blend the mixture until smooth. (An electric mixer can be used but is less efficient).

Whip the cream until fairly stiff and fold into the chocolate mixture.

Divide the mousse among four champagne or parfait glasses and chill for 30 minutes.

FP

Baddeck

"**F**ATHER OF THE TELEPHONE" ALEXANDER GRAHAM BELL, who travelled the world over, maintained that Baddeck, with its tranquil, unspoiled landscape, was the most beautiful place on earth.

Just two years after setting up the Bell Aerial Experiment Association in 1907, Bell was able to witness John McCurdy successfully test fly the Silver Dart, the first plane ever to be flown in the British Empire.

Not only was McCurdy the first man to fly in Canada but he was also the first man to hold a Canadian pilot's license (1910). Fascinated with the science of aviation, McCurdy went on to establish the first aircraft manufacturing factory in Canada. He also served as Lieutenant Governor of Nova Scotia between 1947 and 1952.

The rural area and people around Baddeck appear in the *Memoirs of a Cape Breton Doctor*, written by Cape Bretoner Dr. C. Lamont MacMillan in 1975.

Pilot Casey Baldwin offered Dolly MacLeod a lift one day at Baddeck Bridge. When she hopped in the Silver Dart for a spin, she is believed to have become the first woman ever to fly in an airplane.

Inventor Alexander Graham Bell was involved in another pioneer project — launching the HD-1 in 1911. The development of this type of hydrofoil craft enabled Bell to claim the record for the world's fastest boat in 1919 — a hydrofoil that zoomed across Bras d'Or Lake at 67.8 m/hr.

Baddeck native Michael McLean is responsible for inventing modern fire fighting extension ladders.

In the late 1800s, Mrs. Alexander Graham Bell organized the first Home and School Association in Baddeck. The year 1900 saw the first Montessori School in North America open its doors in Baddeck. A Montessori School stresses freedom of expression and development for its students.

Baddeck native, Casey Baldwin (1882-1948), was the first Canadian to fly a plane. The flight took place in Lake Keuka, New York, in 1908.

Baddeck Scottish Shortbreads
(makes 3 large or 3 dozen small shortbreads)

This recipe was handed down from my husband's Scottish grandmother. These shortbreads are simply delightful. They make a wonderful Christmas gift packed in a colourful tin box or baked in the shape of a small pie, tied with a length of plaid ribbon.

1 lb. butter *454 g*
¼ cup rice flour *50 ml*
1 cup icing sugar *250 ml*
4 - 5 cups white flour *1 L - 1.25 L*
pinch salt

Let butter soften in large bowl.
Add the icing sugar to the butter and beat thoroughly. An electric mixer, especially the kind that will rotate the bowl, works best. If beating by hand, beat at least 5 - 10 minutes. You can't overbeat.
Mix in the rice flour until well combined and add the flour, one cup at a time, until the mixture comes away from the bowl and is firm enough to handle. I find it takes nearly five cups (1.25 L) of flour to reach this stage. One will not need more than five cups (1.25 L) though.
Place the dough in the refrigerator for 30 minutes to make it easier to handle. Divide with a knife into two or three chunks and place one chunk on rolling out surface. Do not be afraid to be rough with it. Using the palm of your hand, slap the dough briskly for 3 or 4 minutes. Gradually shape into a sheet for cutting out cookies or a circle if you wish to make a large traditional shortbread. Ensure that the dough is no less than ½ inch (12 mm) thick. Shape as desired, prick with fork, and bake at 300° F. for about 40 minutes. Watch the shortbread carefully after 30 minutes to make sure the cookies are not browning. Shortbread should be pale yellow in colour.

Note: Butter must be used, and to achieve that melt-in-your-mouth texture, the ingredients must be thoroughly beaten.

Hint: Leave plain or add a festive touch by pressing a pecan half or a maraschino cherry in the centre of each cookie.

F

Barrington

NATIVE INDIANS CALLED THE BARRINGTON AREA "Ministegek" which has the rather obscure meaning "he has gone for it."

This Shelburne County town was the location of the last woolen mill which operated in Canada.

Phil Scott, who gained recognition as a world logrolling champion, is a native of Barrington.

Of historical significance is the "Old Meeting House" in Barrington. Constructed by pre-Loyalists in 1765, it is the oldest non-conformist church building in Canada.

Mrs. Edmund Doane is buried in a Barrington church yard. Her little-known claim to fame is that her grandson penned the words to "Home Sweet Home."

The 4,000 foot **Barrington Passage** to **Cape Sable Island** causeway opened in 1949.

Cape Sable Island was the location of the first Quaker community that settled in Canada (1762).

The popular style of boat known as the Cape Islander is patterned from craft originating at **Clark's Harbour** on Cape Sable Island. The early 1900s designer was Ephraim Atkinson.

Barrington took its name from William Wildman, second Viscount Barrington (1717-1793), Secretary of War in Britain.

Barrington Crackle Top Ginger Cookies
(makes 3 - 4 dozen cookies)

You'll be humming "Home Sweet Home" when you smell these baking in your kitchen. Fragrantly spicy cookies come out of the oven with pretty crackled surfaces, reminding you of the old-fashioned ginger cookies that grandma used to make.

⅔ cup shortening *175 ml*
1 cup sugar *250 ml*
1 egg
¼ cup molasses *60 ml*
2 cups flour, sifted *500 ml*

½ tsp. salt *2 ml*
2 tsp. soda *10 ml*
1 tsp. cinnamon *5 ml*
1 tsp. ginger *5 ml*
¼ tsp. ground cloves *1 ml*

Cream the shortening and sugar. Add the egg and molasses.
Stir the dry ingredients together and add to the shortening mixture.
When well mixed, roll into small balls and dip the tops in sugar. Place two inches (24 mm) apart on ungreased cookie sheet.
Bake for 10 minutes at 350° F. Be careful not to burn.

F

Bedford

THIS THRIVING COMMUNITY AT THE HEAD OF THE BEDFORD Basin was named after John Russell, 4th Duke of Bedford, First Lord of the Admiralty and Secretary of State for the colonies when Halifax was founded.

The father of Stephen Leacock, famed Canadian humourist from Orillia, Ontario, lived many years in Bedford, under the name of Captain James Lewis, dying there in 1940.

Charles Fenerty released to the public in 1844 his invention of paper produced from spruce wood pulp. However, he had already been "beaten to the punch" by German Friedrick Keller who applied for a patent for this type of process in 1840.

Formerly called Fort Sackville, Bedford was also known by the title "Ten Mile House," referring to an inn there where coaches stopped on the route out of Halifax, and was the destination of skating and sleighing parties.

Anthony Holland established on Paper Mill Lake in 1819 one of the first paper mills in Canada.

The Bedford Basin was an awesome sight during the time of World War II, sprinkled as it was with convoys gathered for dangerous treks across the unfriendly waters of the Atlantic Ocean.

The Moir family, who have long been in the bread and chocolate business, opened their first shop in Bedford in 1812. It was a small bakery, operated by Benjamin Moir.

As gestures of his love for Julie St. Laurent, Prince Edward (son of George III), built a heart-shaped pond and a round music room for his companion with whom he lived in Bedford from 1794 to 1800.

The tallest free-standing wedding cake on record for its time (1980) was assembled in Bedford. The forty-eight tier cake, thirty-six feet and six inches tall, was put together by Roy Butterworth and Frank Brennan.

Julie St. Laurent Chocolate Pecan Torte
(serves 8 - 10)

If you can't afford a heart-shaped pond, make this spectacular dessert for someone you love.

⅓ cup butter or margarine *75 ml*
1 cup sugar *250 ml*
4 eggs
1 tbsp. vanilla *15 ml*
6 oz. unsweetened chocolate, melted (6 squares) *175 g*
1¾ cups pecans, finely ground *450 ml*

3 cups strawberries *or* raspberries, fresh or frozen *750 ml*
2 cups whipping cream *500 ml*
¼ cup sugar *50 ml*
1 tsp. vanilla *5 ml*

Preheat oven to 375° F.

Butter one cookie sheet or jelly roll pan and line with buttered wax paper.

Using an electric mixer, cream the butter and sugar until light and fluffy. Beat in the eggs, one at a time. Stir in the vanilla, chocolate and pecans.

Bake for about 20 minutes, watching carefully. The cake should have a fudge-like consistency when removed from the oven. Overbaking will make it crispy and difficult to handle. Carefully remove the cake from the pan onto a rack and peel off the wax paper. Allow it to cool thoroughly and cut the cake in four equal size rectangles.

Whip the cream with the sugar and vanilla until stiff. Spread each cake layer with cream and stack on top of one another. Frost the top and sides with remaining whipped cream. Decorate with semi-sweet or unsweetened chocolate curls. Refrigerate several hours before serving.

Purée raspberries or strawberries in a blender or food processor. If using raspberries, strain the purée to remove the seeds.

Serve each slice of the chocolate pecan torte surrounded by a pool of fruit purée.

Hint: Use a carrot peeler to grate the chocolate from the block.

Note: The cake recipe can be doubled. Use four round pans. You will need more purée but the whipping cream will be enough.

F (unfilled cake only)

Bridgetown

BRIDGETOWN IS ONE OF THE LOVELIEST TOWNS IN THE Annapolis Valley, with its stately, immaculately kept homes.
Not far from Bridgetown was the home of Ernest Buckler, a well-known Canadian novelist and short story writer, who lived there until his death in 1984. Probably his best loved book is *The Mountain and the Valley*, which portrays the life of a young boy growing up in the Annapolis Valley.

Cranberrie Cottage, home of Beatrice Ross Busek, who died in 1985, is a landmark for all those who enjoyed her popular *Connection* cookbook series, and is found in *Granville*.
On Tim Hennigar's farm in this area, Garnet Lewis picked a rare apple in October 1985. One side a brilliant red and the other a deep yellow, it was perfectly split down the middle, half Red Delicious and half Golden Delicious.

New Albany, situated on the other side of the Annapolis River, was the birthplace of Alden Whitman in 1913. Chief obituary writer for the New York Times (1964-1976), he instituted the practice of interviewing public figures before their deaths. In 1980 he published a book called *Come to Judgement* which includes some of the more notable obituaries he wrote.

Endowed with the marvellous name *Paradise*, it is obvious early settlers were impressed by this peaceful spot. In keeping with such a heavenly name, there is an Eden Golf Course nearby.
In 1870, the first cheese factory in Nova Scotia began operation in Paradise.

The 1730 Amberman House in *Granville Ferry*, which is now operated as the North Hills Museum, is a remarkable example of the New England influence in Nova Scotia at that time. The saltbox exterior is typical of that era and the "H" and "L" door hinges, called "Holy Lord hinges," were installed to ward off evil spirits.

The community of *Round Hill* is the site of the grave of Colonel James DeLancey who was better known as "Outlaw of the Bronx" and leader of "DeLancey's Cowboys," who were British partisans during the American Revolution.

Paradise Strawberry Shortcake
(serves 6)

I have been served strawberry shortcake made with sponge cake, pound cake and white cake but still prefer my mother's old-fashioned biscuit version. Cloud biscuits are especially light and provide a pleasant taste and texture contrast to the whipped cream and mashed berries. Truly heavenly!

6 biscuits*
2 cups fresh strawberries, mashed *500 ml*
sugar, to taste
1 cup whipping cream *250 ml*
¼ cup sugar *50 ml*
1 tsp. vanilla *5 ml*

Sweeten the mashed strawberries with sugar to taste.

Whip the cream and add ¼ cup sugar (or less, if preferred) and vanilla.

Split each biscuit in half. Spoon some strawberries on the bottom half, cover with the top half and additional strawberries. Finally, crown the top with a generous dollop of whipped cream.

Note: If you use frozen strawberries, the following thawing procedure retains a fresh taste and pleasing texture in the berries. Separate the berries into clumps and later into individual berries as soon as the thawing process (at room temperature) allows you to (or quickly semi-thaw them in a microwave oven). While still partially frozen, add the desired amount of sugar and mash vigorously.

* *See Cloud Biscuit recipe on page 33.*

M

Halifax

THE FIRST ODDFELLOWS LODGE IN AMERICA WAS ORGANized in 1815 in Halifax.

In 1921, two adventuresome residents of Halifax decided to walk across Canada by following the railway tracks. Shortly after friends Burkman and Carr set out, they were joined by four other Nova Scotians, eager to share the trek. Sid Carr, annoyed, jumped on a train and rode back to Halifax, commenting that he wanted to go for a walk, not a race. The others did make it to Vancouver, although it took them six months.

The first Canadian Volunteer Fire Protection Company was set up in Halifax in 1754.

On June 15, 1983, Diana, Princess of Wales and Prince Charles planted trees on the Halifax Commons to commemorate the International Year of the Child. While the three Canadian Maples and three London Planes were being set out, 200 children strummed ukeleles amid a rainbow of balloons released into the air.

The first divorce court in Canada granted its first divorce in 1750. The Haligonians who were divorced were Lieutenant William Williams and his wife Amy.

The Willow Tree Intersection near the Halifax Commons is so named because it was the location of the "hanging tree" in days gone by. Although the original tree was destroyed, a cutting from it was planted by Princess Margaret during a royal visit.

The very first government lottery held in Canada was in 1752 in order to raise funds for the Sambro lighthouse.

Guiton and Puce were the first cats to cross the Atlantic ocean on a raft (with their owners, of course!). They sailed from Halifax to Falmouth, England, in 1956.

The first occupant of Halifax's handsome Government House was Governor Sir John Wentworth who was Governor between 1792 and 1808. A Loyalist from the American colonies, he had served as Governor of New Hampshire prior to arriving in Canada.

Lieutenant Eileen Vaughan, a Halifax native, became the first female member of the Canadian Forces elitist parachute demonstration team. She joined the "Sky Hawks" in 1986.

Princess Diana Squares
(makes 16 large squares)

Moist, rich and topped with a slightly tart lemon butter frosting, these squares are simply luscious. Fit for a princess!

1 cup dates, finely chopped 250 ml
1 cup boiling water 250 ml
1 tsp. soda 5 ml
¼ cup butter or margarine 60 ml
1 egg, beaten

1 ½ cups white flour 375 ml
½ tsp. salt 2 ml
1 cup white sugar 250 ml
1 tsp. vanilla 5 ml
1 tsp. baking powder 5 ml
½ cup walnuts 125 ml

Combine the first four ingredients and let cool.
Stir in the beaten egg and vanilla.
Mix the dry ingredients together and add all at once to the date mixture. Stir until well combined.
Pour into a well greased 9" by 9" (21 cm by 21 cm) baking pan and bake in a 350° F. oven for 25 - 30 minutes.
Cool thoroughly and frost with the following icing:

¼ cup cream cheese 60 ml
¼ cup butter or margarine 60 ml
2 cups icing sugar 500 ml
½ tsp. lemon extract 2 ml

Cream the cheese and butter together and gradually beat in the icing sugar. Add the lemon extract and beat well.

Note: Princess Diana Squares freeze well, frosting and all.

F

Hantsport

FRANCIS SILVER, WHO IMMIGRATED TO HANTSPORT IN 1861 and lived there until his death in 1920, worked on the estate of a local businessman named Ezra Churchill. Here he indulged his love of painting, making use of every available surface, even basement walls and barn doors. His folk art depicts the seas and sailing vessels, rural landscapes, religious subjects and political cartoons. His work is simple, imaginative, humourous and vivid.

A few miles away lies the settlement of *Falmouth,* home of champion pumpkin grower Owen Woodman. In 1983 his Atlantic Giant pumpkin topped all other entries with its 481-pound weight, while his squash entry weighed 423 pounds.

The first privately owned Canadian railway fruit cars went into operation in Falmouth in 1890.

William Hall, born in *Horton's Bluff* in 1827, was the first Canadian sailor and the first Canadian black to be awarded the Victoria Cross. Hall served briefly on Nelson's flagship "Victory"; he was decorated for bravery in the Crimean War and received the Victoria Cross in 1857 for bravery in action during the Indian mutiny. He returned to his home near *Avonport* where he died in 1904.

Silver Lemon Sherbet
(serves 6 - 8)

For a refreshing dessert, try a scoop of this lemon sherbet on a dewy fresh cantaloupe wedge.

1 cup milk *250 ml*
1 cup sugar *250 ml*
2 lemons
½ cup cream, whipped *125 ml*

Grate the rind off one lemon and squeeze the juice from both lemons.
Whisk the milk, sugar, lemon juice and rind together until sugar dissolves.
Fold in the whipped cream.
Place in the freezer and serve at desired consistency. I prefer it hard and icy while some people like it softer.

Note: For extra tang include the grated rind from the second lemon. Be sure to exclude any of the bitter white pithy layer just under the outer skin.

F

Ingonish

THE PRETTY SETTLEMENT OF INGONISH WAS ONCE KNOWN as "Port of Orleans" and is the home of the beautiful Keltic Lodge resort.

In 1975 Dr. Ronald Nash and his archeological crew discovered the remains of early man on *Ingonish Island*. Estimates place the bones at 7,000 - 8,000 years of age.

In 1497, the first known territorial flag to unfurl in Canada was planted on Sugarloaf Mountain on *Cape North*, the most northerly point on the Cabot Trail.

For visitors to Cape Breton, a must-see is the breathtakingly beautiful Cabot Trail. One of the most exciting points of interest is *Cape Smoky*, a mist-enveloped bluff rising 120 feet above rugged seacoast.

Cape Smoky Special Request Birthday Cake
(makes one large cake)

This superb cake has a wonderful flavour, due to the combination of lemon, vanilla and almond extracts and a highly desirable dense, fine texture. The recipe came from a Cape Bretoner whose family always served it as the traditional birthday cake and each person chose a favorite icing.

1 cup butter 250 ml
2 cups white sugar 500 ml
3 eggs
3 cups cake flour 750 ml
1 tsp. baking powder 5 ml
1 tsp. salt 5 ml
1 cup milk 250 ml
1 tsp. vanilla 5 ml
1 tsp. lemon extract 5 ml
1 tsp. almond extract 5 ml

Cream the butter and sugar together until fluffy. Add the eggs, one at a time, beating well after each addition.
Sift the dry ingredients together and blend into the first mixture.
Stir in the milk and flavourings. Beat until well combined.
Butter and lightly flour a tube pan or a 9" by 13" (21 cm x 33 cm) pan. Pour the batter in and bake in a 325° F. oven for 1 hour.

F

Londonderry

THE COMMUNITY OF LONDONDERRY, ON THE GREAT Village River, was the birthplace of Mrs. G.A. MacIntosh in 1882. This multi-talented lady combined nursing, writing and composing careers and in 1935 wrote "A Song for Nova Scotia."

The unique name of the settlement of *Folly Mountain* is, in fact, a comment on one of its very first settlers, a farmer named Fleming. Apparently, Fleming's efforts to cultivate the land were not obviously successful and the name Fleming's Folly became accepted. Fleming's Folly gradually changed to Folly Mountain.

The first four-masted schooner in Canada, the "J.M. Blackie", was launched in *Great Village* in 1885.

In 1962, Shirley Taggart, at the tender age of fourteen years, broke existing records by picking 450 quarts of strawberries one day at the farm of Charlie Stewart, Great Village. After being paid a special bonus amount of ten cents per box, Miss Taggart was interviewed in the field by the television crew of the show "Country Calendar" and rushed home to get ready for her second job of the day — serving at a strawberry festival supper put on at the local church that evening!

Folly Bars
(makes 2 dozen large squares)

These squares are so delicious and easy to make that they will soon become a family favourite.

> **1 cup brown sugar** *250 ml*
> **1 cup peanut butter** *250 ml*
> **1 cup corn syrup** *250 ml*
> **4 tbsp. butter or margarine** *60 ml*

Mix these ingredients together in a double boiler (or microwave). Stirring frequently, cook gently until the sugar is dissolved.

Remove from heat and stir in:

> **5 cups rice crispies** *1.25 L*
> **1 cup peanuts** *250 ml*

When well combined, spread this mixture into a 9 x 13 inch (21 cm x 33 cm) baking pan. (You may lightly butter the pan, although it really is not necessary.)

Topping:

> 1 square semi-sweet chocolate, melted
> **1 tbsp. butter or margarine** *15 ml*
> **1½ cups icing sugar** *375 ml*
> **½ tsp. vanilla** *2 ml*
> **3 tbsp. hot water** *40 ml*

Beat the topping ingredients together until the desired consistency is reached. You may wish to add a bit more icing sugar.

With a knife, spread the chocolate icing over the rice crispy mixture.

Refrigerate and cut in bars when thoroughly cooled. Store these squares in the refrigerator.

M

"M *Maitland*

"MENESATUNG," THE INDIAN NAME FOR THE MAITLAND area, meant "healing waters." The Lawrence House in Maitland was the home of William D. Lawrence, builder of the largest full-rigged sailing ship in Canada (1874).

Harry and Willard Miller, who were born in **Noel Shore,** were active in the Spanish-American War; in fact, they were the only brother team to win the American Congressional Medal of Honour.

The **Kempt Shore** area was formerly known as the "Man-of-War's Land" due to the many naval officers who were given grants here in the days of early settlement.

Named after Sir Peregrine Maitland, this community on the west side of the mouth of the Shubenacadie River was the home port of the *William Dawson Lawrence*, a 3-masted windjammer, the first of its kind to be built in Canada. A massive vessel, the *W.D. Lawrence* had a deck measuring 242 feet, 6 inches in length. Her keel was 244 feet, 9 inches long; her mainyard, 90 feet; and her main mast, 200 feet and 8 inches. She weighed 3,800 tons and was rigged with 8,000 yards of sail. This magnificent ship cost its builder $107,000, a very handsome sum in 1874.

In the early decades of the nineteenth century, the only shoe peg factory in Canada to be in full operation was that of Lewis and Sons, which was located in **Stewiacke**.

Stewiacke has the distinction of being situated exactly midway between the Equator and the North Pole.

Noel Shore Orange Christmas Cake
(makes two large cakes)

This cake has a different flavour from the usual light fruitcakes abundant during the Christmas season. Try it — you'll love it.

1½ cups sugar *375 ml*
1 cup butter or margarine, softened *250 ml*
3 eggs, beaten
1½ cups crushed pineapple *375 ml*
½ cup pineapple juice *125 ml*
2 tsp. lemon extract *10 ml*
2 tsp. almond extract *10 ml*
2¾ cups flour *675 ml*

2 tsp. baking powder *10 ml*
1 tsp. nutmeg *5 ml*
2 cups light raisins *500 ml*
¾ cup orange peel, grated* *200 ml*
1 cup maraschino cherries, halved *250 ml*
1 cup coconut, shredded *250 ml*
¼ cup mixed candied peel, chopped *50 ml*

* *Three oranges should yield the required amount.*

Cream the butter and sugar together and add the beaten eggs, crushed pineapple, pineapple juice and the lemon and almond extracts, and mix well.

Sift together the flour, baking powder and nutmeg.

Mix the dry ingredients into the liquid mixture until well combined. Fold in the raisins, peel, cherries, grated orange peel and coconut. Spoon into well-greased and floured pans. Bake at 300° F. for about 2 hours.

B FP F

North Sydney

IN 1920 NORTH SYDNEY WAS ASTIR BECAUSE THE *PERMANICIA* was being launched. This unique vessel was Canada's first concrete boat.

The World Snipe Championship was held in North Sydney in 1979.

Ferry service between North Sydney and Newfoundland was established in 1898.

The well-loved Ferris Hill Toboggan Slide in North Sydney was once reputed to be the best "slide" between here and Montreal.

The first propane plant in Nova Scotia commenced operation at **Leitches Creek** in 1950.

Little Bras d'Or native, George Rice, was the official photographer of the Greely Polar Expedition in 1883. Unfortunately, Rice lost his life in this courageous venture to the Far North.

Coxheath native Ken Langley broke all records when he accompanied Gary Sowerby of Moncton on a car trip around the world. Their "Odyssey 1977" saw them cover 27,000 miles in seventy-four days and eleven minutes.

Well-known folk singer and musician John Allan Cameron was born in the Cape Breton community of **Port Hood** in 1938 and was raised in **Mabou**.

Mr. and Mrs. Rinus Van de Ven of **Judique** are the proud parents of the first quadruplets ever recorded to be born in Nova Scotia. These babies came into the world at the Grace Maternity Hospital in Halifax in 1979. Two boys and two girls, the youngsters have grown to be good-looking, happy, healthy and very active.

Coxheath Chocolate Chip Goodies
(makes 2 ½ dozen)

These would be great to have along on a 74-day car ride! They are my husband's absolute favourites and he considers himself a chocolate chip cookie connoisseur!

½ cup shortening *125 ml*
½ cup white sugar *125 ml*
¼ cup brown sugar *60 ml*
1 egg
2 tsp. vanilla *10 ml*

1 cup flour *250 ml*
½ tsp. baking soda *2 ml*
¼ tsp. salt *1 ml*
1 cup semi-sweet chocolate morsels *250 ml*

Cream the sugars with the shortening. Add the egg and vanilla, and mix well.
Combine the flour, soda and salt and add all at once to the shortening mixture. Mix well and stir in the chocolate chips.
Grease the baking sheets with shortening.
Either drop the dough with a teaspoon on the baking sheets or roll in walnut sized balls (if you wish a more uniform shape).
Cook in a preheated 375° F. oven for 8 to 10 minutes.

Note: Do not use an electric mixer in this recipe — as the cookies may lose their shape when baking. Also, do not substitute whole wheat flour for white flour. I have tried it and the results were disastrous!

F

North West Range

THE LUNENBURG COUNTY COMMUNITY OF NORTH WEST Range is the site of the North West Range Meeting House. Its first pastor, Joseph Dimock, born in *Newport* in 1770, was the first native born Baptist minister ordained in Canada and was very prominent in organizing the Baptist mission in Nova Scotia. On view in the Meeting House is the original glass communion set and a brass spittoon which is placed near the pulpit. It is thought that the first two people in Nova Scotia baptized by immersion were members of Joseph Dimock's congregation.

In 1828, six North West Range Baptist ladies walked forty miles to Wolfville to cast their votes in favour of the founding of Horton Academy (now Acadia University). Proud of their appearance and of undeniably strong stock, these hardy women walked barefoot all the way to Wolfville to save their shoes for their encounter with society folk.

North West Range Butterscotch Squares
(makes 16 squares)

These tasty squares are moist and buttery. They freeze well.

¼ cup butter or margarine *60 ml*
1 cup brown sugar *250 ml*
2 eggs
¾ cup flour *200 ml*
1 tsp. baking powder *5 ml*
½ cup chopped nuts *125 ml*

Place the butter and brown sugar in a saucepan and stir over medium heat until caramelized (until the sugar is completely dissolved into the butter).

Remove from heat and let cool. Then beat in the eggs, flour, baking powder and nuts.

Spread this mixture in a greased 9 x 9 inch (21 cm square) pan and bake at 350° F. 15 to 17 minutes. Cool.

Ice with the following frosting:

2 tbsp. butter or margarine *30 ml*
½ cup brown sugar *125 ml*
2 tbsp. milk *25 ml*
1½ cup icing sugar *375 ml*

Place the brown sugar and butter in a pan and bring to a boil on the stove. Add the milk and let come to a boil again. Take the mixture off the stove and add the icing sugar, beating until it is of the right spreading consistency.

While the icing is still warm, ice the squares using a knife dipped in hot water to achieve a smooth, shiny surface. Using a toothpick, decorate the icing with diagnonal lines going from one corner to the other. Turn the pan and draw lines in the other direction so that they crisscross each other. Cut in squares and serve.

Orangedale

WHEN FIRST SETTLED, THIS TINY INVERNESS HAMLET WAS without a name until the population grew to the point where it was decided it was about time they had a proper address. No one seemed able to come up with a name, except one inhabitant, who happened to be an Irish "Orangeman." Appropriately, he suggested the name of Orangedale which was received favourably by his comrades and has remained unchanged to the present time.

Micmac artist Madeline Knockwood (1899-1974) was born in **Malagawatch**, near Marble Mountain, Inverness County. Using fragile pieces of pliable wood dyed soft, natural colours, she fashioned intricately patterned, realistic-looking flowers. Her apple blossoms, water lilies and dozens of other species are collectors' items. Fortunately, she taught this unique craft to several students who still practise it.

Orangedale Squares
(makes 2 dozen squares)

Orangedale squares have a sweet, tart flavour and chewy texture.

1 cup butter or margarine 250 ml
2¼ cups sugar 550 ml
2 cups flour 500 ml
¾ tsp. orange peel, grated 3 ml
4 eggs
½ cup orange juice 125 ml
½ tsp. baking powder 2 ml
1 tbsp. icing sugar 15 ml

Cream the butter and ½ cup (125 ml) sugar in a large bowl. Stir in 1¾ cups (450 ml) flour and the orange peel. When the mixture resembles crumbs, press it into a 13 x 9 inch (33 cm x 21 cm) pan. Bake at 350° F. for 20 minutes.

While the bottom layer is baking, blend the eggs, the remaining 1¾ cup (425 ml) sugar, the remaining ¼ cup (60 ml) flour, juice and baking powder. If you do not have an electric mixer to help you here, make sure you beat this until well combined.

Pour this over the baked bottom layer and return to the oven to bake for another 25 minutes. When done, let sit in the pan until thoroughly cool. Sprinkle with icing sugar and cut into squares.

Hint: These freeze well, but sprinkle with icing sugar *after* they have been removed from the freezer and have reached room temperature.

F

Parrsboro

THE BEAUTIFUL COMMUNITY OF PARRSBORO ON THE MINAS Basin takes its name from John Parr, who was Governor of Nova Scotia between 1782 and 1791.

The first airmail received and sent in eastern Canada was flown in and out of Parrsboro in 1919.

Parrsboro was the first town in Canada to own its own electrical plant, which opened in 1899.

The *M.V. Kipawo,* a 123-foot car and passenger ferry used in the Minas Basin and Newfoundland waters from 1926 to 1977, was the oldest continuously operating car ferry in Canada. The *Kip* plied the route between Parrsboro, **Kingsport,** and Wolfville, with a capacity for carrying 120 passengers and nine automobiles.

In 1985, the biggest fossil find in North America was unearthed on the north shore of the Bay of Fundy's Minas Basin, about six miles east of rural Parrsboro. This scientific gold mine consisted of more than 100,000 pieces of 200-million-year-old fossils and is described as the largest single collection of fossils. It is the first such collection found in North America and the first fossils of that age discovered outside of South Africa. A unique part of the extensive find is a series of dinosaur footprints the size of a penny, which are the smallest ever known on earth.

Fox River, which empties into Greville Bay, is the home of John Chipman Kerr, who was born here in 1887. Kerr was awarded the Victoria Cross for outstanding bravery in World War I.

The **Minas Basin** has achieved world fame for its incredibly high tides. High and low tides in the Basin range from forty-seven and one-half feet to a maximum of fifty-three and one-half feet.

In 1919, the Handley-Page bomber Atlantic made a crash landing in Parrsboro. This was quite an event for the community as the Handley-Page was the largest aircraft in the world at that time and much interest was generated in the craft's progress through repairs and the successful completion of its flight to New York.

Parrsboro Pecan Pie
(makes one pie)

Pecan pie lovers will be especially pleased with this recipe because it is surprisingly quick and easy to make.

½ **cup butter or margarine** *125 ml*
⅔ **cup brown sugar** *175 ml*
1 cup shelled pecans *250 ml*
3 eggs, well-beaten
2 tsp. vanilla *10 ml*
¾ **cup corn syrup** *200 ml*
1 unbaked pie crust*

Cream the butter and sugar together until light and fluffy.
Add the corn syrup, eggs, vanilla and beat well. Stir in the pecans and pour the mixture into a pie shell.
Bake at 400° F. for 10 minutes. Reduce the temperature to 350° F. and bake for 30 minutes longer.
Serve garnished with sweetened whipped cream.

Hint: To add a special touch, scatter about ¾ cup (225 ml) of chocolate chips in the pie shell and pour the pecan filling over them. The chocolate melts during baking and you end up with a creamy layer on the bottom. I call this version "Black Bottom Pecan Pie."

* *See Pugwash Perfect Pie Crust, p. 112.*

Preston

NORTHEAST OF DARTMOUTH, PRESTON IS THE OLDEST black community in Canada and is the home of the first Black Cultural Museum in Canada.

When 500 Maroons from Jamaica arrived in Halifax in 1796, they settled in the Preston area and were instrumental in the construction of the Citadel Hill fortifications. However, they did not find the harsh climate to their liking and left "en masse" for Sierra Leone.

In the early 1800s, the Preston area was resettled by blacks escaping to Nova Scotia from the American colonies under protection of British warships.

Richard Preston, a great religious leader and personal friend of the renowned slavery abolitionist, William Wilberforce, was responsible for organizing the African Baptist Association in 1854. However, Preston was not named after Richard Preston but after a Captain Preston who was involved in the granting of land parcels in the Preston area in its initial days of settlement.

Preston Blueberry Delight
(serves 10 - 12)

This dessert feeds a crowd. Although the squares are not very thick, they are rich and satisfying.

Crust:

½ cup margarine, melted *125 ml*
2 cups graham wafers crushed (about 25 wafers) *500 ml*
2 tbsp. sugar *25 ml*

Cream Centre:

1 large package cream cheese
½ cup sugar *125 ml*
1 tsp. vanilla *5 ml*
2 eggs

Blueberry Topping:

4 cups blueberries (fresh or frozen) *1 L*
¾ cup sugar *200 ml*
2½ tbsp. cornstarch *37 ml*
1 tsp. cinnamon *5 ml*
¼ tsp. nutmeg *1 ml*
½ tsp. lemon juice *2 ml*

Mix together the crust ingredients and press into a 13 x 9 inch (33 cm x 21 cm) pan.

Cream the cheese with the sugar. Add the eggs and vanilla. Beat until smooth and pour over crumb crust. Bake at 350° F. for 15 - 20 minutes.

Combine all ingredients for the blueberry topping in a saucepan and bring to a boil. Cook until thickened and remove from heat. Cool a bit before pouring over the cream cheese layer in the pan.

Refrigerate.

Serve with a mound of whipped cream on each portion.

B FP

Pugwash

At one time called Waterford, the unusual name of Pugwash is derived from the Indian word "pugwesk," meaning "shallow water." The street names in this pretty Cumberland County town are posted in both English and Gaelic, reflecting the Scottish heritage of its inhabitants. One of Pugwash's native sons became a world known figure. He was Cyrus Eaton, who was born here in 1883. One of the most powerful industrialists in North America, Eaton was highly respected in financial circles where he became known as the "Merger Sphinx." Mr. Eaton was also an humanitarian and was instrumental in organizing the first Pugwash Thinkers' Conference on Science and World Affairs in 1957. This peace and awareness conference continues to draw experts in all fields from all over the world and is now held in various locations around the globe.

Oxford was at one time called "Slabtown" because of its many sawmills which produced large quantities of slabwood. Located at the junction of Black River and River Philip, researchers are of two minds on how the community got its name. Some claim it was named after the famous English University and others say it is due to the fact that oxen were able to ford the river in this area.

Born in Oxford at the turn of the century, Margaret Fulton Beatty made her mark in the world as a talented artist, critic, lecturer and author.

Pugwash Perfect Pie Crust
(enough for one 2-crust pie)

2 cups flour *500 ml*
1 tsp. salt *5 ml*
²/₃ cup shortening (chilled) *175 ml*
2 tbsp. butter or margarine (chilled) *30 ml*
4 tbsp. ice water *60 ml*

Sift the flour and salt together.

Cut the shortening and butter into the flour with a pastry cutter or two knives. When the mixture resembles coarse meal, sprinkle with ice-cold water and mix with a fork lightly. At this point, you may find it necessary to add a bit more water.

The dough should form readily into a ball which should be refrigerated until ready to use.

Flour a rolling-out surface and use a floured rolling pin. By turning the dough frequently, you will be able to roll out the dough without having it stick to the rolling surface. Gently wrap the dough around the pin and unroll it directly into a pie plate, pleating the rim with your fingers and trimming the excess dough from the edges with a sharp knife.

Hint: *To ensure perfect crust every time:*

Sift the flour — this allows it to combine quickly with the fat.

Use chilled fats. You may wish to substitute lard for the shortening.

Make sure the water for mixing is ice-cold. I usually place a couple of ice cubes in a small dish of water a few minutes before using it.

Do not overhandle the dough or it will be tough instead of flaky.

Flour the rolling pin and the rolling out surface to prevent the crust from sticking, but do not add too much flour or you will spoil the texture of the dough.

When making a two-crust pie, brush the top lightly with milk to get a delicately browned crust.

Bake the unfilled shells in a preheated 450° F. oven for about 10 minutes or until lightly browned.

F (baked or unbaked)

Sandy Cove

SANDY COVE WAS THE HOME OF LAURENCE BRADFORD Dakin, a journalist, novelist and poet and probably one of the most learned Greek and Roman scholars of his time. He could speak six languages and read nine. Born in 1904, he died in 1972.

The mysterious "Jerome" was found in Sandy Cove in 1861. Abandoned on the beach with both legs amputated and wearing "fine linen," Jerome lived in Digby County for forty-seven years, apparently without uttering a word to clear up the mystery of his origins. It was said he would speak to children but would never respond to any questions put to him by visitors who attempted to communicate with him in various languages.

Amos M. Smith of **Little River** had an illustrious boxing career in Canada and the United States. A fisherman's son, he became the first native-born Canadian to win the world welterweight title (1892) and was also the first officially recognized champion in the welterweight division. This talented boxer fought under the professional title, the "Mysterious Billy Smith."

The area around Sandy Cove was called Prince William until 1850. When you have visited the fine, sandy beaches here, it is easy to see where it got its present name.

Westport, on the eastern side of Brier Island, was the home of adventurer Joshua Slocum, the first man to sail around the world alone. Born in North Mountain in 1844, he spent most of his "on land" time in Westport. His great voyage began on April 24, 1895, and ended on June 27, 1898, when he completed his circumnavigation of the globe. The three-year trek of 46,000 miles in a little craft called the *Spray* (36'9" long) was an admirable feat for anyone, let alone a man in his 50s. A skilled storyteller, he left behind three books: *Sailing Alone Around the World, Voyage of the Destroyer,* and *Voyage of the Liberdale.*

Digby Neck Fudge Brownies
(makes 2 dozen large brownies)

This recipe comes from a long-established "Neck" family who feel it's the best brownie recipe in any "neck of the woods." The chocolate icing melts into the brownies, sealing in their moistness. They are truly delicious and freeze well.

1 cup margarine *250 ml*
2 cups sugar *500 ml*
5 tbsp. cocoa *75 ml*
4 eggs, beaten
1 cup flour *250 ml*
1 cup walnuts, chopped *250 ml*
2 tsp. vanilla *10 ml*

Cream the sugar, cocoa and margarine together. Stir in the beaten eggs and vanilla. Mix in the flour and fold in the walnuts.

Place the batter in a greased 9 by 13 inch (21 cm x 33 cm) pan and place in a 350° F. oven for 40 to 45 minutes. The brownies may appear underdone but they should not be cooked any longer as they will become too dry.

As soon as the brownies are removed from the oven, frost them with the following chocolate icing and decorate with a few more chopped walnuts, if desired.

Icing:

2 cups icing sugar *500 ml*
2 tbsp. cocoa *30 ml*
2 tbsp. margarine *30 ml*
2 tbsp. boiling water *30 ml*
2 tsp. vanilla *10 ml*

Mix the icing with an electric mixer or beat by hand until well blended.

F

Sydney

WILLIAM KNAPP BUCKLEY, A NATIVE OF SYDNEY, GAINED international recognition as a druggist. Perhaps his best known concoction is "Buckley's Cough Mixture."

Sydney-born Eric LeBlanc set a new Canadian weight lifting record in 1980 for lifting 1,140 pounds total in three lifts.

In 1918 the "Motion Picture Classic" magazine proclaimed Wallace MacDonald the "King of Charm." Few people realized the "King of Charm" started his career in Sydney where his first job was a junior Royal Bank clerk.

The first legal police strike in Canada took place in Sydney in 1971.

The Honourable John Buchanan, Premier of Nova Scotia, was born in Sydney, and has served as premier in his home province since 1978.

A war veteran by the name of Verner, who was wounded at Vimy Ridge, came home to Sydney where he became involved in designing fire escape equipment for hospitals. His pioneer work in this specialized area was an important step in promoting safety awareness measures in public buildings.

The first Canadian horse hospital was opened in Sydney in 1900.

Former hockey defenceman Allister MacNeil, the first Nova Scotian to coach a Stanley Cup winner (the Montreal Canadiens), hails from Sydney. He was also the only coach at that time to lead his team to consecutive Stanley Cup (NHL) and Calder Cup (AHL) championships.

The first black lawyer in Canada, Delos Davis, was a native of Sydney.

Sydney-born Parker MacDonald, a respected hockey professional, scored thirty-three goals as a Detroit Red Winger.

Danny Gallivan, the well-known "Voice" of the Montreal Canadiens hockey team was born in Sydney. Gallivan actually started his career as a baseball pitcher with the New York Giants in 1939. However, his switch to broadcasting was a well-chosen one, earning him the ACTRA Sportscasting Award in 1974.

If you are interested in breeding New Zealand white rabbits, the man to see is Joseph Filek of Sydney. Mr. Filek set a Guiness world record when his rabbit produced a litter of twenty-four baby bunnies.

Referred to as the "Steel City," Sydney's Dominion Steel and Coal Company at Whitney Pier is the largest self-contained steel plant in North America.

Named after the early explorer, John Cabot, the strategic Cabot Strait waterway was the scene of a disaster when the oil tanker *Kurdistan* split in half here on March 15, 1979, in pack ice, 16 nautical miles northeast of Sydney. Most of the 25,000 tonnes of Bunker C oil aboard was saved by salvagers who towed the stern section ashore. The bow was towed 230 miles out from the coast and sunk by the Canadian Navy.

One of Canada's best loved poets, Robert William Service (1874-1958), spent two years working in the Barclay Bank on the corner of Archibald Avenue and Commercial Street in North Sydney.

During World War II, the Sydney Harbour was earmarked as an alternate site for United Kingdom Headquarters, should the Allied effort in Europe fail.

The news of Admiral Robert Peary's (1856-1920) discovery of the North Pole was broadcast to the world from the Western Union Cable Office in North Sydney in 1909.

A native of North Sydney, the Honourable George Murray was premier of Nova Scotia from 1896 to 1921, holding the record for longest tenure in that office.

Sydney Carrot Cake
(makes one tube pan cake)

If your spirits need "bucking up," try a generous slice of Sydney Carrot Cake.

1 cup sugar *250 ml*
1 cup vegetable oil *250 ml*
3 eggs, beaten
½ tsp. salt *2 ml*
1⅓ tsp. baking soda *6 ml*
1⅓ tsp. baking powder *6 ml*
1⅓ tsp. cinnamon *6ml*
1⅓ cups flour *325 ml*
2 cups carrots, grated *500 ml*
½ cup walnuts, chopped *125 ml*

Dissolve the sugar in the oil and stir in the eggs. Combine the salt, soda, baking powder, cinnamon and flour and incorporate into the oil mixture. Add the carrots and nuts and mix until well combined.

Pour the batter into a well greased tube pan and bake it 1¼ hours at 300° F.

Cool and ice with Cream Cheese Icing.

This icing recipe is very generous; you may wish to cut it in half if you plan to ice only the top of the cake.

Cream Cheese Icing:

1 large package cream cheese
¼ cup butter or margarine *60 ml*
3 cups icing sugar *750 ml*
2 tsp. vanilla *10 ml*
2 tbsp. walnuts, chopped *30 ml*

Cream the cheese and butter together in a mixing bowl. Add the icing sugar and beat well. Stir in vanilla.

Ice the cake and sprinkle with the two tablespoons of walnuts.

Note: This cake can be frozen — although you probably won't have any left to freeze!

F FP B

Sydney Mines

LOCATED ON THE NORTH SIDE OF SYDNEY HARBOUR, THE Cape Breton town of Sydney Mines has a rather amusing story in its past. It seems that many people used to call Sydney Mines "Lazytown," a name it got from farmers bringing their produce to market early each summer morning. Apparently the miners left for work at dawn and their wives got up to prepare a hearty breakfast for them, returning to bed for more sleep after their husbands left. Consequently, whenever the farmers' wagons rolled into town, they were greeted by drawn shades and no signs of life and the standing joke was that no one in Sydney Mines got up early.

A native son of Sydney, long-distance runner Johnny Miles won the Boston Marathon on April 19, 1926, setting a new record. Not content with one victory, he won the Marathon again in 1929.

The first dial telephone system in Canada was instituted in Sydney Mines in 1907. However, there were too many "bugs" to be worked out and telephones reverted to the old manual style until 1939 when a dial system was re-introduced, this time to stay.

As early as 1672, when Nicolas Denys published his *Description of Natural History of the Coast of North America,* the presence of coal was noted here.

For over two centuries, Sydney's coalfields were Canada's major producer of coal and accounted for one-third of the continent's annual coal production until 1960.

Lazytown Chocolate Fluff
(serves 4-6)

Lazytown Chocolate Fluff is a longtime favourite in our house and you will find it a snap to prepare. It has a true chocolatey taste and is especially good served warm. The recipe yields a generous amount of chocolate sauce to spoon over the rich dark chocolate cake.

½ **cup white sugar** *125 ml*
2 **tbsp. shortening** *30 ml*
2 **tbsp. cocoa** *30 ml*
2 **tsp. baking powder** *10 ml*
1 **cup flour** *250 ml*
½ **tsp. salt** *2 ml*

½ **cup warm milk** *125ml*
½ **cup brown sugar** *125 ml*
3 **tbsp. cocoa** *45 ml*
2 **cups boiling water** *500 ml*
1 **tbsp. butter or margarine** *15 ml*

Cream the sugar with the shortening until fluffy.

Sift 2 tbsp. (30 ml) of cocoa, baking powder, flour and salt together.

Add the warm milk to the shortening mixture and stir in the flour mixture. When well combined, place the dough in a casserole dish or loaf pan.

Mix 3 tbsp. (45 ml) of cocoa and brown sugar together and sprinkle over the batter.

Dissolve the butter in the hot water and pour over the batter.

Bake at 350° F. for 40 minutes.

Wallace

Located at the mouth of the Wallace River, this community was originally called "Ramshack" or "Ramsheg." Renamed in 1810, it was named after one of these two men: Honourable Michael Wallace, Lieutenant Governor of Nova Scotia (1818-1824) or Sir William Wallace, a national Scottish hero.

Simon Newcomb, who was born in Wallace in 1835, was a world famous astronomer and inventor who was involved in a wide range of projects, from being the first man to calculate the speed at which light travels to developing air-conditioning units. He published over 500 works on astronomy, mathematics and economics, received honorary degrees from ten European and seven American universities, was a member of forty-five foreign societies, and the recipient of numerous prizes and awards. When elected in 1907 to the New York Hall of Fame, he was the only Canadian-born person to be so honoured. He was also appointed a Rear Admiral of the U.S. Navy. Albert Einstein said of Simon Newcomb, "If it had not been for the work of Simon Newcomb, I would not have been."

Stone from the large sandstone quarries in the Wallace area was used to build Province House and the Parliament Buildings in Ottawa.

Adeliza Betts was a Wallace native who patterned her life after her heroine, Florence Nightingale. Although her tombstone reads simply, "Adeliza A. — 1853-1934", Miss Betts was one of the greatest humanitarians ever to devote her life to the healing of the sick, especially the poverty-stricken. She was primarily responsible for organizing the New England Deaconess Hospital, which grew from a staff of three nurses to a fully-equipped, modern institution, respected across the nation. An interesting note is that Adeliza's mother, Philopina Atkinson Betts, a pioneer in her own right, was the first woman ever to teach public school in Nova Scotia.

Wallace Butter Pecan Custard Cream
(serves 4)

If you enjoy homemade ice cream but don't own an ice cream maker, this recipe is an excellent alternative. The pecans add a pleasant crunch to the smooth, rich custard cream.

4 egg yolks	1½ tsp. vanilla *7 ml*
1½ cups milk *375 ml*	1 cup cream, whipped *250 ml*
⅛ tsp. salt *.5 ml*	¾ cup pecans, coarsely
½ cup white sugar *125 ml*	chopped *200 ml*
	3 tbsp. butter *45 ml*

Whisk the egg yolks, milk, salt and sugar together in the top of a double boiler over bubbling hot water or use your microwave oven. Cook this mixture until it coats the back of a spoon. Stir in the vanilla. Cover and chill thoroughly in the refrigerator.

In a saucepan, melt the butter and sauté the pecans in it until they are golden. Cool.

Remove the custard mixture from the refrigerator and fold in the whipped cream and the nuts. Freeze until just firm.

Spoon into parfait glasses and serve with small, dainty cookies.

Note: Custard cream freezes well but tastes creamier if allowed to soften up a bit in the refrigerator (after removing from the freezer) before serving.

F M

Wolfville

LOCATED IN FERTILE FARMLAND, WOLFVILLE HAS AN abundance of delicious fresh fruit, harvested during the summer and fall. Wolfville Fresh Fruit Pie will be one of your favourites.

This pretty town, which boasts one of the world's smallest natural harbours, is the home of Acadia University, formerly known as Queen's College.

Originally called Mud Creek, townsfolk soon decided on a new name, Wolfville, in honour of outstanding local citizens of the surname deWolfe.

At nearby **Horton**, the first Baptist ordination in Canada took place. In 1778, the Reverend Nicholas Pearson became an ordained Baptist minister.

Alex Colville, a world famous realist painter, makes his home in Wolfville. Technically flawless and executed with the unerring hand of the gifted artist, Colville's works are much sought after by art collectors everywhere.

The Kipawo Showboat Company, organized by Acadia University's Professor Jack Sheriff, is a local theatrical group, often performing socially conscious plays penned by Professor Sheriff himself. The Company takes its name from the ferry which, in early days, used to travel between Kingsport, Parrsboro and Wolfville.

Entrepreneur and prominent Nova Scotian businessman Roy Adelbert Jodrey was born in 1889 in **White Rock**, an area close to Wolfville. Jodrey's biography by Harry Bruce is simply called *R.A.* A "wheeler and dealer" who thrived on the intricacies of money making, the stock market and the philosophy of good hard work, this self-styled millionaire patterned his life on the adage: "Money may be used to give warmth for a moment or planted like an acorn to give shade forever." Until his death in 1975, "R.A." believed in Nova Scotia and made successes of local enterprises when other businessmen were leaving the Maritimes to make their fortunes in greener fields to the west or south.

The first garden club in Nova Scotia was formed in Wolfville in 1935 with Mrs. Mary Forbes as President.

Watson Kirkconnell (1895-1977) served a lengthy term as president of Acadia University from 1958-1964. One of Canada's most prolific and learned scholars, this brilliant man was adept at translating fifty languages into English.

Greenwich, an area just outside Wolfville, has many orchards and a spectacular view of Blomidon. Early settlers called it "Noggins Corner" but it was later renamed Greenwich after the Connecticut town which itself was named after the famous British observatory town on the Thames River.

Wolfville Fresh Fruit Pie
(makes 6-8 smallish servings)

This is an exceptionally easy recipe. You will be pleased at the fresh berry taste of the pie.

4 cups raspberries *or* strawberries *1 L*
3 tbsp. cornstarch *45 ml*
2 tbsp. lemon juice *30 ml*
1 cup sugar *250 ml*
1 baked pie crust*

Pick over the berries and wash.
Combine half the berries with cornstarch, lemon juice and sugar in a saucepan. Cook over medium heat, stirring frequently, until thickened. Cool.
Gently stir in the remaining berries. Pour into a baked pie crust and chill. Serve with whipped cream or ice cream.

* *Use Pugwash Perfect Pie Crust recipe, p. 112.*

York Redoubt

ONE OF THE FIVE MARTELLO TOWERS IN THE HALIFAX AREA is located in the picturesque park at York Redoubt. The other four fortification towers were built on McNab's Island, Point Pleasant Park, Fort Clarence, and George's Island.

There are two plausible reasons for the name *Herring Cove:* Tom Herring was an early settler, and the Cove was once alive with herring.

The Thrumcap Shoals off Herring Cove spelled disaster for the *HMS Tribune*, a vessel with 250 people on board. *The Tribune* sank here one stormy night in November 1797. Ten passengers managed to stay afloat until the next morning; however, none of the villagers would risk their lives in the violent sea to rescue the survivors. Finally, a thirteen year-old boy named Joseph Shortt took out a skiff and brought two of the nearly dead men to shore. His courage inspired some of the adults to action and all ten survivors were brought safely ashore.

A member of the Canadian Sports Hall of Fame, Herring Cove native George Brown (1839-1875) was a North American professional sculling champion. A strong, able fisherman, Brown had the endurance necessary to compete in the demanding rowing championships locally and internationally.

McNab's Island, which guards the entrance to Halifax Harbour, was originally called Cornwallis Island. Offered for sale in May 1773 for 1,000 pounds sterling, it was sold to Peter McNab, a navy lieutenant who had served with Cornwallis and who happened to be the brother-in-law of renowned Haligonian Joseph Howe. McNab purchased it on Christmas Day in 1782 and it was renamed McNab's Island. Destined to play a strategic role in defending Halifax's harbour, the island became the site of Fort McNab. Erected on a hill which had once served as the McNab family burial ground, the fortifications, built in the late 1800s, cost 24,000 pounds. This money came from profits Britain had made from operations of the Suez Canal.

Known as the "King of Smugglers," Joseph Mauger started things brewing in Halifax when he operated a smuggling business on MacNab's Island in the mid 1700s.

York Redoubt Chocolate Chip Cheesecake
(serves 10-15)

No doubt about it, this cheesecake always gets rave reviews and it is so rich that a little goes a long way. A great party cake!

1½ cups cream-filled chocolate cookies finely crushed *375 ml*	2 tsp. vanilla *10 ml*
¼ cup margarine, melted *60 ml*	1 cup chocolate chips *250 ml*
3 large packages cream cheese, softened	1 tsp. flour *5 ml*
1 can sweetened condensed milk	1 cup whipping cream *250 ml*
3 eggs	

Preheat oven to 300° F.

Combine the chocolate cookie crumbs and margarine. Pat firmly into the bottom of a large springform pan.

In a large mixer bowl, beat the cheese until fluffy. Add the milk and beat until smooth. Add the eggs and vanilla, mixing well.

In a small bowl, toss the chips together with the flour and then stir into the cheese mixture. Pour into the prepared pan. Sprinkle a few additional chips over the top.

Bake one hour or until the cake springs bake when lightly touched.

Cool to room temperature before removing the sides of the pan.

Serve with whipped cream garnished with chocolate curls.

Note: This cheesecake is equally good served without the whipped cream and simply accompanied by cups of steaming hot coffee.

B FP

Recipe Index

A

Amherst Old Fashioned Cream Puffs 88
Annapolis Royal Apple Squares 90
Appetizers Canning Chicken Liver Pâté 4
  Grand Narrows Sausage Rolls 9
  Grand Garlic Dip 12
  Port Morien Mussel Kabobs 20, 21
  Sable Island Shrimp Pâté 22
  Special Stellarton Stuffed Mushrooms 25
  Tangier Smoked Salmon Bites 23
Apples Annapolis Royal Apple Squares 90
  LaHave Appled Cabbage 42

B

Baddeck Scottish Shortbreads 93
Banook Stuffed Spareribs 62
Barley Dunvegan Barley Casserole 35
Barrington Crackle Top Ginger Cookies 94
Bayfield Ripe Tomatoes at Their Best 3
Beans Truro Green Bean Bake 52
Bear River Cherry Blossom Loaf 31
Beef Super, Natural Meatloaf 67
  Lake Ponhook Beef Casserole 68
Berwick Potato Flan 32
Best Yarmouth Seafood Chowder, The 27
Blueberries Nappan Blueberry Muffins 45
  Preston Blueberry Delight 111
Bluenose Mushroom Soup 8
Breads Bear River Cherry Blossom Loaf 31
  Glen Margaret Oatmeal Brown Bread 47
  Halifax Hovis Bread 37
  Weymouth Savory Loaf 54
Brussels Sprouts Maverick Great Brussels Sprouts 39

C

Cabbage LaHave Appled Cabbage 42
  New Glasgow Marinated Cole Slaw 19
Cakes Cape Smoky Special Request Birthday Cake 102
  Julie St. Laurent Chocolate Pecan Torte 96
  Noel Shore Orange Christmas Cake 105
  Sydney Carrot Cake 116
  York Redoubt Chocolate Chip Cheesecake 122
Canning Chicken Liver Pâté 4
Canso Cloud Biscuits 33
Cape Smoky Special Request Birthday Cake 102
Carrots Sydney Carrot Cake 116

Cherries Bear River Cherry Blossom Loaf 31
Chicken Canning Chicken Liver Pâté 4
    Little Egypt Chicken 80
    Tatamagouche Bay Herbed Chicken Breasts 75
Chocolate Coxheath Chocolate Chip Goodies 106
    Julie St. Laurent Chocolate Pecan Torte 96
    Lazytown Chocolate Fluff 117
    Spencer's Island Chocolate Mounds 86
    St. Peter's Chocolate Mousse 91
    York Redoubt Chocolate Chip Cheesecake 122
Cookies Baddeck Scottish Shortbreads 93
    Barrington Crackle Top Ginger Cookies 94
    Coxheath Chocolate Chip Goodies 106
    Spencer's Island Chocolate Mounds 86
Corn Whycocomagh Baked Corn 57
Cornwallis Fruit Salad 6
Coxheath Chocolate Chip Goodies 106
Cucumbers Glace Bay Cucumber Salad 11

D

Digby Neck Fudge Brownies 114
Digby Scallops Crème de la Crème 64
Dingle Dumplings 39
Duck Pinkney Point Roast Duck 60, 61
Dunvegan Barley Casserole 35

F

Folly Bars 103, 104
Fruit Annapolis Royal Apple Squares 90
    Bear River Cherry Blossom Loaf 31
    Cornwallis Fruit Salad 6
    Nappan Blueberry Muffins 45
    Noel Shore Orange Christmas Cake 105
    Orangedale Squares 108
    Paradise Strawberry Shortcake 98
    Preston Blueberry Delight 111
    St. Ann's Spicy Baked Fruit 50
    Silver Lemon Sherbet 99
    Wolfville Fresh Fruit Pie 120

G

Glace Bay Cucumber Salad 11
Glen Margaret Oatmeal Brown Bread 47
Good Cheer Vegetable Medley 49
Grand Garlic Dip 12
Grand Narrows Sausage Rolls 9

H

Halifax Hovis Bread 37

Ham Pictou Pineapple Glazed Ham 79
Heart of the Valley Marinated Salad 17

J

Julie St. Laurent Chocolate Pecan Torte 96

K

Kejimkujik Spinach Soup 15

L

LaHave Appled Cabbage 42
Lake Ponhook Beef Casserole 68
Lamb Port Mouton Rack of Lamb 77
Lazytown Chocolate Fluff 117
Lemon Silver Lemon Sherbet 101
Little Egypt Chicken 80
Liverpool Saucy Salmon Loaf 70
Louisbourg Seafood Casserole 71
Lunenburg Baked Rice 44

M

Mahone Bay Mussels 73
Maverick Great Brussels Sprouts 39
Muffins Nappan Blueberry Muffins 45
       Windsor Pumpkin Muffins 56
Mushrooms Bluenose Mushroom Soup 8
       Special Stellarton Stuffed Mushrooms 25
Mussels Mahone Bay Mussels 73
       Port Morien Mussel Kabobs 20, 21

N

Nappan Blueberry Muffins 45
New Glasgow Marinated Cole Slaw 19
Noel Shore Orange Christmas Cake 105
North West Range Butterscotch Squares 107

O

Orangedale Squares 108
Oranges Noel Shore Orange Christmas Cake 105
       Orangedale Squares 108

P

Paradise Strawberry Shortcake 98
Parrsboro Pecan Pie 110
Pasha Rice 41
Pâté Canning Chicken Liver Pâté 4
   Sable Island Shrimp Pâté 22

Pecans Parrsboro Pecan Pie 110
    Wallace Butter Pecan Custard Cream 119
Pictou Pineapple Glazed Ham 79
Pies Parrsboro Pecan Pie 110
    Pugwash Perfect Pie Crust 112, 113
    Wolfville Fresh Fruit Pie 120
Pinkney Point Roast Duck 60, 61
Pork Banook Stuffed Spareribs 62
    Pictou Pineapple Glazed Ham 79
    Springhill Stuffed Pork Chops 83
Port Morien Mussel Kabobs 20, 21
Port Mouton Rack of Lamb 77
Potatoes Berwick Potato Flan 32
Preston Blueberry Delight 111
Princess Diana Squares 100
Pugwash Perfect Pie Crust 112, 113
Pumpkin Windsor Pumpkin Muffins 56

R

Raspberries Wolfville Fresh Fruit Pie 120
Rice Lunenburg Baked Rice 44
    Pasha Rice 41

S

Sable Island Shrimp Pâté 22
St. Ann's Spicy Baked Fruit 50
St. Peter's Chocolate Mousse 91
Salads Bayfield Ripe Tomatoes at their Best 3
    Cornwallis Fruit Salad 6
    Heart of the Valley Marinated Salad 17
    Glace Bay Cucumber Salad 11
    New Glasgow Marinated Cole Slaw 19
Salmon Liverpool Saucy Salmon Loaf 70
    Tangier Smoked Salmon Bites 23
Sausages Grand Narrows Sausage Rolls 9
Scallops Digby Scallops Crème de la Crème 64
Seafood Digby Scallops Crème de la Crème 64
    Liverpool Saucy Salmon Loaf 70
    Louisbourg Seafood Casserole 71
    Mahone Bay Mussels 73
    Port Morien Mussel Kabobs 20, 21
    Sable Island Shrimp Pâté 22
    Shelburne Baked Sole 81, 82
    Tangier Smoked Salmon Bites 23
    The Best Yarmouth Seafood Chowder 27
Shelburne Baked Sole 81, 82
Shrimp Sable Island Shrimp Pâté 22
Silver Lemon Sherbet 101

Sole Shelburne Baked Sole 81, 82
Soups Bluenose Mushroom Soup 8
    Town Clock Chunky Tomato Soup 14
    Kejimkujik Spinach Soup 15
    The Best Yarmouth Seafood Chowder 27
Special Stellarton Stuffed Mushrooms 25
Spencer's Island Chocolate Mounds 86
Spinach Kejimkujik Spinach Soup 15
Springhill Stuffed Pork Chops 83
Squares Annapolis Royal Apple Squares 90
    Digby Neck Fudge Brownies 114
    Folly Bars 103, 104
    North West Range Butterscotch Squares 107
    Orangedale Squares 108
    Princess Diana Squares 100
Strawberries Paradise Strawberry Shortcake 98
    Wolfville Fresh Fruit Pie 120
Super, Natural Meatloaf 67
Sydney Carrot Cake 116

T

Tangier Smoked Salmon Bites 23
Tatamagouche Bay Herbed Chicken Breasts 75
Tomatoes Bayfield Ripe Tomatoes at their Best 3
    Town Clock Chunky Tomato Soup 14
Town Clock Chunky Tomato Soup 14
Town Crier Turnip Puff 37
Truro Green Bean Bake 52
Turnips Town Crier Turnip Puff 37

V

Veal Valiant with Mushroom Sauce 66, 67
Vegetables Bayfield Ripe Tomatoes at their Best 3
    Berwick Potato Flan 32
    Glace Bay Cucumber Salad 11
    Good Cheer Vegetable Medley 49
    Heart of the Valley Marinated Salad 17
    Kejimkujik Spinach Soup 15
    LaHave Appled Cabbage 42
    Maverick Great Brussels Sprouts 40
    New Glasgow Marinated Cole Slaw 19
    Sydney Carrot Cake 116
    Town Clock Chunky Tomato Soup 14
    Town Crier Turnip Puff 38
    Truro Green Bean Bake 52
    Whycocomagh Baked Corn 57
    Windsor Pumpkin Muffins 54

W

Wallace Butter Pecan Custard Cream 119
Weymouth Savory Loaf 54
Whycocomagh Baked Corn 57
Windsor Pumpkin Muffins 56
Wolfville Fresh Fruit Pie 120

Y

York Redoubt Chocolate Chip Cheesecake 122

Place Name Index

A

Advocate 86
Albion Mines 24
Albro Lake 61
Amherst 87, 88
Annapolis Royal 89, 90
Antigonish 2
Arcadia 60
Arichat 91
Auburn 32
Auld Cove 2
Avonport 99
Aylesford 32

B

Baddeck 92
Baleine Cove 71
Barrington 94
Barrington Passage 94
Barton 63
Bayfield 2
Bear River 30, 31
Bedford 95
Berwick 32
Bible Hill 52
Birchtown 82
Blomidon Lookoff 3
Bras d'Or Lake 68
Bridgetown 97
Bridgeville 24
Burnside 7, 61

C

Camp Aldershot 16
Canning 3, 4
Canso 33
Cape Blomidan 3
Cape Forchu 26
Cape North 102
Cape Sable Island 94
Cape Smoky 102
Cerberus Rock 91
Chaswood 23
Chebucto Head 37
Chester 72

Chester Basin 72
Cheticamp 34
Chipman's Corner 41
Church Point 55
Clementsport 5, 6
Clementsvale 5
Clark's Harbour 94
Coxheath 106
Crow Harbour 33

D

Dartmouth 7, 61,
Deep Brook 5, 6
Digby 63
Dunvegan 34

E

East Mapleton 81
East Pubnico 60
East River 23
Englishtown 50
Eskasoni 9

F

Fairview 13
Falmouth 99
Folly Mountain 103
Fox River 109

G

Glace Bay 10
Glen Margaret 46
Grand Narrows 9
Grand Pré 11, 12
Grande Anse 91
Granville 97
Granville Ferry 97
Great Village 103
Greenwich 120
Guysborough 2

H

Hackett's Cove 46

Halifax 13, 36, 38, 40, 65, 66, 99
Hall's Harbour 41
Hantsport 101
Herring Cove 121
Horton 119
Horton's Bluff 99

I

Imperoyal 61
Ingonish 102
Ingonish Island 102
Inverness 57

J

Joggins 44
Jordan Falls 82
Judique 106

K

Kejimkujik 15
Kempt Shore 104
Kentville 16
Kingsburg 42
Kingsport 109

L

LaHave 42
Lake Ainslie 57
Lake Micmac 61
Lake Ponhook 68
Lake Rossignol 68
Lake Wallace 68
Leitches Creek 105
Lequille 89
Little Bras d'Or 105
Little Egypt 79
Little River 113
Liverpool 69
Lockeport 82
Londonderry 103
Louisbourg 71
Lunenburg 43

M

Mabou 106
Maitland 104
Mahone Bay 72

Malagash 74
Malagawatch 108
Mapleton 81
Margaree Forks 34
Marriott's Cove 72
Marshalltown 63
McNab's Island 121
Milton 76
Minas Basin 109
Moose River 23

N

Nappan 44
New Albany 97
New Annan 74
New Glasgow 18
New Ross 16
Newport 107
Noel Shore 104
North Sydney 105, 115, 116
North West Range 107
Northeast Margaree 34

O

Oak Island 72
Orangedale 108
Ovens 42
Oxford 112

P

Paradise 97
Parrsboro 109
Peggy's Cove 46
Pictou 78
Pine Lake 68
Pinkney Point 60
Port Hood 106
Port Morien 20
Port Mouton 76
Port Royal 48
Port Wallace 61
Port Williams 3
Preston 110
Pugwash 44, 112

R

River John 79
Rood's Head 82
Round Hill 97

S

St. Ann's 50
St. Peter's 91
Sable Island 21
Sandy Cove 113
Sheet Harbour 22
Shelburne 80, 81
Shubenacadie Canal 7
Smith's Cove 5
Spencer's Island 86
Springhill 82, 83
Stellarton 24
Stewiacke 104
Sunnyside 66
Surette Island 60
Sydney 115
Sydney Mines 117

T

Table Head 20
Tangier 22, 23
Tatamagouche Bay 74
Trenton 18
Truro 51
Tufts Cove 61

U

Upper Clements 5

V

Victoria Beach 48

W

Wallace 118
Waterville 32
Welsford 41
Westphal 61
Westport 113
Weymouth 53, 54
White Rock 120
Whycocomagh 57
Windsor 55, 56
Windsor Junction 24
Wolfville 109, 119, 120
Woodlawn 7, 61
Woodside 61

Y

Yarmouth 26, 27
York Redoubt 121

List of Illustrations

Page 5 — Private Peter Byrne (1943).
From the Private Collection of Mr. Peter Byrne

Page 8 — Dr. Helen Creighton
From the Private Collection of Dr. Helen Creighton

Page 17 — The Mackay Car.
Courtesy of the Nova Scotia Museum

Page 24 — The "Samson", Pictou County's first coal-burning locomotive.
Courtesy of the Public Archives of Nova Scotia

Page 30 — Watson Peck demonstrating the proper stance for canoe tilting.
From the Private Collection of Mr. Watson Peck

Page 34 — Cheticamp Hooked Rug.

Page 45 — The Nappan Experimental Farm of yesteryear.
Courtesy of Agriculture Canada

Page 46 — William Black, the Nova Scotian "Father of Methodism."
Courtesy P.A.N.S.

Page 49 — The "Habitation" at Port Royal.
Courtesy of P.A.N.S.

Page 51 — Portia White.
Courtesy of P.A.N.S.

Page 53 — Amor de Cosmos

Page 55 — Sam Langford
Courtesy of P.A.N.S.

Page 64 — Halifax's Town Clock on historic Citadel Hill.
Courtesy of Tourism Halifax

Page 73 — The "Sea Chest" — summer retreat for author and diplomat, Charles Ritchie.
From the Private Collection of Mrs. E.W. Finch-Noyes

Page 74 — Jost Vineyards Wine Label.

Page 76 — Margaret Marshall Saunders with pet dog "Billy Sunday."
Courtesy of P.A.N.S.

Page 89 — Annapolis Tidal Power Generating Station.
Courtesy of the Nova Scotia Power Corporation

Page 92 — Mr. and Mrs. Alexander Graham Bell.

Page 95 — Julie St. Laurent.
Courtesy of P.A.N.S.

Bibliography

Bannerman, Jean. *Leading Ladies — Canada*, Mika Publishing Co., 1977.
Bird, Will R. *Off Trail in Nova Scotia*, Toronto, Ryerson, 1956.
———— *This is Nova Scotia*, Toronto, Ryerson, 1950.
Brown, Brenna and Jeremy. *Book of Canadian Winners and Heros*, Toronto, Prentice-Hall Canada Inc., 1983.
Brown, Thomas J. *Nova Scotia Place Names*, [Halifax, N.S. Royal Print and Litho, 1922].
Bruce, Harry. *R.A. — The Story of R.A. Jodrey*, Toronto, McClelland and Stewart, 1979.
Cameron, James M. *More About Pictonians*, Hantsport, Lancelot Press, 1983.
CanExpo Publishers Inc. *Quick Canadian Facts*, Surray, CanExpo Publishers Inc., 1983.
Cassidy, Ivan. *Nova Scotia/All About Us*, Scarborough, Nelson Canada, 1983.
Colombo, John Robert. *Canadian Literary Landmarks*, Willowdale, Houndslow Press, 1984.
———— *Colombo's Little Book of Canadian Proverbs, Graffiti, Limericks and Other Vital Matters*, Edmonton, Hurtig Publishers, 1975.
Creighton, S.F. *Colchester County — A Pictorial History*, Oxford. 1979.
DesBrisay, Mather Byles. *History of the County of Lunenburg*, Bridgewater, Bridgewater Bulletin Ltd., 1967.
Donovan, Kenneth, Editor. *Cape Breton at 200*, Sydney, University of Cape Breton Press, 1985.
Duffus, Allan; MacFarlane, Edward; Pacey, Elizabeth; Rogers, George. *Thy Dwellings Fair: Churches of Nova Scotia*, Hantsport, Lancelot Press, 1982.
Elliott, Shirley B. *N.S. Book of Days*, Halifax, Nova Scotia Communications and Information Centre, 1979.
Engel, Marian. *The Islands of Canada*, Edmonton, Hurtig Publishers, 1981.
Fox, Brent. *Camp Aldershot: Serving Since 1904*, Kings Historical Society, 1983.
Fraser, Mary L. *Folklore of Nova Scotia*, Antigonish, Formac Ltd.
Fergusson, Charles Bruce. *Place Names and Places of Nova Scotia*, Halifax, Public Archives of Nova Scotia, 1967.
Hall, E. Foster. *Heritage Remembered — The Story of Bear River*, Bear River New Horizons Centre, Bear River, 1981.
Hamilton, William B. *Local History in Atlantic Canada*, Toronto, MacMillan Co. of Canada Ltd., 1974.
———— *The MacMillanBook of Canadian Place Names*, Toronto, MacMillan, 1978.
Harris R.V., Q.C. *A Brief History of St. George's Church*.
Hashey, Mary W. *Maritime Artists, Volume I*, Fredericton, Maritime Arts Association, 1967.
Heritage Trust of Nova Scotia. *Lakes, Salt Marshes and the Narrow Green Strip*, Halifax, 1979.
Hill, Daniel G. *The Freedom Seekers — Blacks in Early Canada*, The Book Society of Canada Ltd., 1981.
Hilts, Len. *Guide to Canada*, Rand McNally and Co., 1977.
Kallman, Helmut, Editor, *Catalogue of Canadian Composers*, Toronto, Garden City Press Co-Operative, 1951.
Major, Marjorie. *From the Ground*, Halifax, Petheric Press Ltd., 1981.

Marble, Allan E. *Nova Scotians at Home and Abroad,* Windsor, Lancelot Press, 1977.

Mitcham, Allison. *Offshore Islands of Nova Scotia and New Brunswick,* Hantsport, Lancelot Press, 1984.

Mosher, Edith. *From Howe to Now,* Hantsport, Lancelot Press, 1981.

Newton, Pamela. *Cape Breton Book of Days,* University of Cape Breton Press, 1984.

North Cumberland Historical Society. *Some North Cumberlandians,* 1965.

─────── *Some North Cumberlandians at Home and Abroad Past and Present,* 1985.

Nova Scotia Museum, Nova Scotia Department of Education. *Museums in Nova Scotia,* 1985.

Nova Scotia Department of Tourism. *Nova Scotia — Where to Stay, What to See, Where to Eat, What to Do,* 1986.

Pacey, Elizabeth, editor. *The Prince and Hollis Buildings,* Heritage Trust of Nova Scotia, Halifax, 1976.

Powell, R. Baden. *Scrap Book — Digby Town and Municipality.*

─────── *Second Scrap Book — Digby Town and Municipality.*

Quinpool, John. *First Things in Acadia,* Halifax, First Things Publishers Ltd., 1936.

Rasky, Frank. *Great Canadian Disasters,* Toronto, Longmans Green and Co., 1961.

Readers Digest Association (Can.) Ltd. *Readers Digest Canadian Book of the Road,* 1980.

─────── *Scenic Wonders of Canada,* 1976.

Rogers, George, editor, Nova Scotia Association of Architects. *Exploring Nova Scotia 1,* Halifax, Formac Publishing Co. Ltd., 1984.

Russell, Loris. *Everyday Life in Colonial Canada,* London, B.T. Batsford, 1973.

Sampson, Gordon H.; Currie, Donna Anderson. *North Bar Remembered,* City Printers Ltd., 1985.

Shand, Gwendolyn Vaughan. *Historic Hants County,* Halifax, 1979.

Sherwood, Roland H. *Legends, Oddities and Facts from the Maritime Provinces,* Hantsport, Lancelot Press, 1984.

Stephens, David E. *Truro — A Railway Town,* Hantsport, Lancelot Press, 1981.

Sylvestre, Guy; Conron, Brandon; Klenik, Carl. *Canadian Writers,* Ryerson, 1964.

Tolson, Elsie Churchill. *The Captain, the Colonel and Me.* Sackville, N.B., Tribune Press Ltd., 1979.

Toye, William, Editor. *Oxford Companion to Canadian Literature,* Toronto, Oxford University Press, 1983.